Introduction to Airline and Airport Management

Introduction to Airline and Airport Management

Fifth Edition

James Edmunds

Harlow, England • London • New York • Boston • San Francisco • Toronto • Sydney • Auckland • Singapore • Hong Kong
Tokyo • Seoul • Taipei • New Delhi • Cape Town • Sao Paulo • Mexico City • Madrid • Amsterdam • Munich • Paris • Milan

Pearson Education Limited
Edinburgh Gate
Harlow
Essex CM20 2JE

And associated companies throughout the world

Visit us on the World Wide Web at:
www.pearson.com/uk

First published 2009
This edition published 2015 by Pearson Education Limited

ISBN 978-1-78448-048-6

Printed and bound in Great Britain by Clays Ltd, Bungay, Suffolk.

Introduction to Airline & Airport Management

Welcome to this fifth edition (updated 2015) of this key text Introduction to Airline & Airport Management. The aim of this text is to help support you undertake Level 4 (Foundation Degree and undergraduate Degree) aviation management studies. The text will also act as an excellent reference source for your continued studies at level 5 and 6 of any airline and airport management undergraduate programme. The aim of this text is also to support those students who have entered postgraduate studies within the area of commercial aviation management but have no previous knowledge of the subject area.

The text aims to help you achieve the following:

- To provide an understanding of the nature, structure and organisation of the airline & airport industry.

- To examine the key developments within airline and airport sectors

- To explore the relationship between public and private sector organisations within international aviation.

- To focus on the component sectors of the industry and their operating characteristics.

This text is broken down into twelve sections that roughly translate into the areas that you will cover over the period of your studies.

The areas that we will be covering are outlined below:-

- Introduction to Commercial Aviation

- Historical Overview of Commercial Aviation

- The Airline and Airport Industry (broken down into two distinct sections)

- The Airline Product

- Aviation Technology

- Commercial Aviation Aircraft Manufacturers

- Airport Operations

- Aviation Law

- Commercial Aviation Regulatory Bodies

- Careers in Commercial Aviation

- The Future of Flight

You should look at completing the reading and tasks before you attend the class. The text can also be used as a reference guide and will be a vital revision aid for future tests and recapping your knowledge as your studies progress.

It is important to remember that no text can be comprehensive enough to replace your class time and therefore it is essential that you attend all sessions.

I hope that you benefit from using this study aid and that you enjoy learning about commercial aviation which is one of the world's most dynamic and exciting industries to both study and work within.

James Edmunds

Contents

Unit One

Introduction to Commercial Aviation Management

Unit Objectives:

On completing this unit, you should be able to:

- Discuss the difference between military, commercial and general aviation
- Illustrate understanding of the key concepts and terminology used within commercial aviation
- Understand the main airport and airline codes utilised within commercial aviation

Definition of Commercial Aviation

The term aviation covers the entire array of organisations involved with flight. This ranges from government organisations including the military through to private pilots owning their own light aircraft. The term civil aviation is often used to describe the airline and airport business, however, this term also encompasses both commercial and private (general aviation) operations. Therefore, within this study guide we will refer specifically to Commercial Aviation see fig 1.1.

Fig 1.1 – The Aviation Industry

Sector	Military Aviation	Commercial Aviation	General Aviation
Purpose	Fighter and bomber operations Logistics	Passenger operations Cargo operations Logistics	Passenger operations Leisure flights
Infrastructure	Airbases	Airports	Airports and airfields

As can be seen from figure 1.1, the term military aviation covers all aspects of flight that deal specifically with the defence of a country. Military aviation tends to use exclusive facilities which are often prohibited to the general public due to national defence issues. The airspace above military establishments may also be 'off limits' to all other forms of aviation.

The development of commercial aviation has had a profound impact on the economy and society. Global aviation is currently weathering an unprecedented array of macroeconomic impacts. These negative economic events include:

- The Eurozone crisis – Countries which have signed up to the single European currency – the Euro- are finding it difficult to balance their countries books due to crises in their financial systems. Countries currently affected include Greece, Spain, Cyprus, Portugal, Italy and Ireland. This turmoil has reduced employment and required countries to reduce spending. The implications for this have impacted on air travel with less people able to fly from these countries and reduced the number of passengers wishing to travel to these areas due to the

4

threat of strikes and civil disobedience. Here the demise of carriers such as Cyprus Airways can be directly attributed to the problems associated with recession.

- Oil Price – The price of oil to the commercial aviation sector has decreased by roughly 40% year-on-year. This is a sizable reduction and has created a number of challenges for airline managers. Lower oil prices mean more competition, as Full Service Network Carriers (FSNC) are able to use this price reduction as leverage in their fares against Low Cost Competition. Whilst it may not lead to parity in their fares it will help reduce them making them more appealing to customers to use FSNC services. At the time of writing (May 2015) a barrel of Brent Crude Oil costs roughly $65. This is a significant reduction on the 2014 average price of $100 and much lower than the $180 per barrel recorded in 2008.
- Economic gloom in the United States and China – The world's two most powerful economies are also struggling due to the economic malaise. This global uncertainty has reduced the number of passengers flying and airline profitability.

In 2014 some 3.3 billion passengers flew (up 5.5% on the previous year), on over 33 million flights with this figure expected to increase to 3.5 billion in 2015 (Source: International Air Transport Association - IATA). Despite the economic gloom the industry remained profitable in 2014 achieving $19.9 billion.

Fig 1.2 – Global Airline Net Post-tax profitability

Year	Profit/Loss ($ Billion)
2013	10.6
2014	19.9
2015 (est)	25.0

Source: IATA

Commercial aviation management has a vital role to play within the global economy. Aviation directly employs over 8.7 million, in 2014, according to Air Transport Action Group (ATAG). When looking at total employment contribution (both direct and indirect) related to commercial aviation this figure grows to over 58 million. By 2030, this figure is forecasted to increase above 83 million, with most of these jobs being generated within the Asian economic area, more specifically China. Air currently transports over 35% of all world trade amounting to $5.3 trillion by value.

The shape of commercial aviation is undergoing significant change with commentators believing that products such as First Class travel requiring major overhaul if they are to survive in the portfolio of services offered. The phenomenal growth of Low Cost Carriers continues unabated with the Asian market currently seeing an explosion of new entrant airlines based on a cost focused business strategy.

The term commercial aviation will be used within this text to describe any air journey for which the passenger/cargo has paid to use the service. The rapid development of airports and airlines to cater for commercial air transport will be discussed within the text as will the different types of operator which have been created to service this need.

Finally the term general aviation is applicable to the private use of aviation resources. Within this category we can include the use of private aircraft, balloons and micro lights.

Key Terms and Concepts

The commercial aviation industry uses a variety of terminology, abbreviations and technical jargon to help speed up the administration processes. This section of the text looks at covering the main areas and sets you to work in finding out certain aspects for yourself.

The Phonetic alphabet

An accurate and easy to understand radio communication method for both short and long distance communication, this method of telecommunications is used extensively within aviation operations. The phonetic alphabet replaces the sound of letters with specific names therefore allowing accurate information to be passed between staff. The full phonetic alphabet is highlighted below:-

A	Alpha	N	November
B	Bravo	O	Oscar
C	Charlie	P	Papa
D	Delta	Q	Quebec
E	Echo	R	Romeo
F	Foxtrot	S	Sierra
G	Golf	T	Tango
H	Hotel	U	Uniform
I	India	V	Victor
J	Juliet	W	Whisky
K	Kilo	X	X-ray
L	Lima	Y	Yankee
M	Mike	Z	Zulu

Information: At Atlanta Hartsfield-Jackson International Airport the term Delta is replaced by 'Dixie' so as not to cause confusion with the main carrier operating at this airport Delta Airlines. In numerous areas of the world Foxtrot is also replaced by the term 'Fox' as it is easier to pronounce.

Airport and Airline Codes

Anyone who has travelled by air will know how the sector has created its very own language. The use of codes to identify airports, airlines, radio beacons, cargo pallets etc has allowed the industry to develop highly efficient systems to allow passengers, their luggage and cargo to get from A to B efficiently, correctly and, probably, most importantly on-time. The main driving force behind the customer facing system is the International Air Transport Association (IATA). The three letter code for airports and the two letter airline codes that we are all accustomed to have been developed by this trade body. Whilst using the IATA system is part and parcel of the everyday lives' of employees within the commercial aviation industry, they will also be expected to understand and use the International Civil Aviation Organisations (ICAO) four letter airport and three letter airline codes if they are involved in route planning or navigation. The difference between these two systems can be seen in fig 1.2 which shows the coding for London Heathrow Airport and British Airways.

Fig 1.2 – Airline & Airport Codes

	IATA Coding	ICAO Coding
Heathrow - Airport Code	LHR	EGLL
British Airways - Airline Code	BA	BAW

Task 1

Can you identify the following airport codes by looking at www.world-airport-codes.com

IATA	~~IATA~~ Name	ICAO	City	Country	FHA
ABZ	Aberdeen Dyce	EGPD	Aberdeen	UK	
AMS	Amsterdam Schiphol	EHAM	Netherlands → Amsterdam		
ARN	Stockholm-Arlanda	ESSA	Stockholm	Sweden	
BAH	Bahrain International	OBBI	Manama	Bahrain	
BCN	Barcelona Int. Airport	LEBL	Barcelona	Spain.	
BHX	Birmingham Int. Air.	EGBB	Birmingham	UK.	
BRS	Bristol Int.	EGGD	Bristol	Uk	
CPH	Copenhagen Kastrup	EKCH	Copenhagen	Denmark.	
DFW	Dallas Fort Worth Int.	KDFW	Dallas-Fort-Worth	U.S	
EDI	Edinburgh	EGPH	Edinburgh	UK.	
FCO	Leonado Da Vinci Int.		Rome	Italy	
GLA	Glasgow Int.	EGPF	Glasgow	UK.	
HKG	H.K. Int. Airport	VHHH	Hong Kong	Hong Kong	
ISB	Benazir Bhutto Int.	OPRN	Islamabad	Pakistan	
LAX	Los Angeles Int.	KLAX	Los Angeles	US	
LCY	London City Airport	EGLC	London	UK	
LGW	London Gatwick Air.	EGKK	London	UK.	
MAN	Manchester	EGCC	Manchester	UK	
MIA	Miami Int.	KMIA	Miami	US	
NCL	Newcastle	EGNT	Newcastle	UK	
PRG	Ruzyně Int. Airport	LKPR	Prague	Czech Republic	
SFO	San Francisco Int.	KSFO	San Francisco	US	
STN	London Stansted	EGSS	London	UK	
SYD	Sydney Kingsford Smith Int.	YSSY	Sydney	Australia	
YVR	Vancouver Int.	CYVR	Vancouver	Canada	
ZRH	Zürich Airport	LSZH	Zurich	Switzerland	

Task 2

Can you identify the following airline codes by looking at www.airlinecodes.co.uk

AA	American Airline Inc.
AC	Air Canada
BA	British Airways p.l.c
ET	Ethiopian Airlines Enterprise
FR	Ryanair Ltd.
IB	Iberia Lineas Aereas de Espana S.A. Operadora
KE	Korean Air Lines Co. Ltd.
LH	Deutsche Lufthansa AG LH220 / Lufthansa Cargo AG
LY	El Al Israel Airlines Ltd.
NB	Skypower Express Airways Ltd.
OA	Olympic Air
QF	Qantas Airways Ltd.
U2	Easyjet Airlines Company Limited
UL	SriLankan Airlines Limited
VS	Virgin Atlantic Airways Limited.

Aviation Abbreviations

The use of abbreviations within aviation is common place. The list below is just a sample of some of these abbreviations that you will come across whilst working within the commercial aviation sector:-

A/C	Aircraft
ATB	Automatic Ticket and Boarding Pass (e-Ticket)
ATC	Air Traffic Control
BCBP	Bar Coded Boarding Pass
BST	British Summer Time
CAA	Civil Aviation Authority
CANX	Cancelled
CHD	Child
CSA	Customer Service Agent
CUSS	Common Use Self Service
CUTE	Common Use Terminal Equipment
ETA	Estimated Time of Arrival
ETD	Estimated Time of Departure
FAA	Federal Aviation Administration
FFP	Frequent Flyer Programme
FL	Flight Level
FQTV	Frequent Traveller
GMT	Greenwich Mean Time
IATA	International Air Transport Association
ICAO	International Civil Aviation Organisation
IFE	In Flight Entertainment
ILS	Instrument Landing System
INF	Infant (under two years of age)
JAR-OPS	Joint Aviation Requirement Operations
MCO	Miscellaneous Charges Order

N/S	Night Stop
NDB	Non-Directional Beacon
PAX	Passenger
PNR	Passenger Name Record
SFU	Suitable For Upgrade
STA	Scheduled Time of Arrival
STBY	Standby
STD	Scheduled Time of Departure
TBA	To Be Advised
TCA	Traffic Conference Area
TOD	Ticket On Departure
U/S	Unserviceable
ULD	Unit Load Device
VOR	Very High Frequency Omni-Directional Radio Beacon

Commercial Aviation Terminology

There follows a brief description of the main terminology used within commercial aviation management. Most of the terms relate directly to the operational aspects of a flight and airport operations. You will find that other areas of the industry will have their own nomenclature. 命名法.

- **Air Traffic Control** – The role of ATC is broken down into a number of disciplines. 有紀律 The primary function of air traffic control is to separate aircraft thus avoiding the possibility of mid air collisions. 沖突 ATC is also, however, responsible for the smooth flow of air traffic across their sector and to provide pilots with essential information to help support the flight. The two main sections of ATC are Airport Control (including clearance and approach controllers) and en-route control. The first ATC system was introduced at London's Croydon airport in the early 1920's. In the UK, air traffic is co-ordinated by the National Air Traffic Service (NATS) which is owned 49% by the government and the rest by major UK airlines including British Airways, Virgin, easyJet and Lufthansa German Airlines.

- **Airbridge/Jetty** – A flexible link between the aircraft and the terminal building. The use of air bridges allows for safe and quick embarkation and disembarkation of an aircraft and take-off 起飞 Landing protects passengers from the elements whilst undertaking this process.

- **Airline Alliances** – Cooperation agreements signed by airlines which can cover a variety of operational and management functions including marketing and maintenance. The three main commercial alliances are Star, Skyteam and Oneworld.

Task 3

Identify the airlines that make up the airline alliances of Star, Skyteam and Oneworld? 聯盟

Lufthansa
Air China
China Southern

Star Alliances — Singapore Airlines

Skyteam
Vietnam Airlines   Korean Air

Cathay Pacific Incl. Dragonair

Oneworld — Japan Airlines

BA

Qatar Air (new)

- **Airways** – The routes (corridors) used by aircraft to navigate successfully from A to B. The maps illustrating airways resemble, in some respects, the motorway system used by motor vehicles. Each airway is named as are motorways (for example Green One links London to Wales, Ireland and onwards to the start of the North Atlantic Oceanic tracks) with the lines linking radio beacons along the flight path.

- **Apron/Ramp** – The apron is an area of the airport where aircraft will park to allow passengers and cargo to get on and off. It is whilst on the apron/ramp that all the service vehicles will undertake the necessary operations to make the aircraft serviceable again. This will include catering supplies, water, fuel, and sanitary operations as well as cargo and luggage functions.

- **Auxiliary Power Unit** – The Auxiliary Power Unit or APU as it is commonly referred to, is a engine mounted normally in an aircraft's tail. Its purpose is to supply power to the craft when the main engines are switched off and there is no available ground power.

- **Cockpit** – The nerve centre of an aircraft's operations. It is here that the pilots will sit to operate the flight from departure to arrival. Today's cockpits are filled with modern LCD panels and computers which have helped take a certain amount of the burden off the crew. Most modern civilian aircraft will have a two man cockpit made up of a captain and first officer (co- pilot). However, on certain aircraft such as the Boeing 777-300 which undertake long haul, flights the cockpit crew can be made up of four pilots (two captains and two first officers) who will take it in turns to fly the plane. Whilst not in command, the crew can utilise a room linked to the cockpit which has bunk beds for them to rest in.

- **Extended-Range Twin-Engine Operational Performance** – ETOPS is the certificate awarded to twin engine aircraft that allows them to fly over oceans. Aircraft that can be classified within this operational category are the Boeing 757, 767, 777 and 787 or the Airbus A330, A350. Depending on the ETOPS rating awarded, these aircraft will be allowed to fly 180 minutes or more away from a diversionary airport. Lately the use of smaller Airbus A318 or Boeing 737 aircraft have been drafted into this category for use on all-business class routes – British Airways for example, offers flights on-board Airbus A318's between London City and New York's JFK. Such certificates are not awarded to aircraft with four engines, such as; the Boeing 747 or Airbus A380, as the chances to all four engines catastrophically failing together is remote. This situation is however changing and all aircraft will be ETOPS rated from 2016.

- **Holding point** – The point at which an aircraft must wait until being cleared by Air Traffic Control to enter a runway or taxiway.

- **Hub and Spoke** – A system of interconnected airports that allows passengers to reach their final destination by transferring aircraft at large international 'hub' airports such as London Heathrow or Dallas Fort Worth. The concept of hub and spoke has helped airlines increase their market share and efficiency as they are able to serve more destinations by using such techniques. The Hub and Spoke system originally developed in the US by traditional carriers such as United and American Airlines has expanded across the globe and is an essential element within the airline alliance system.

Task 4

Draw the typical Hub and Spoke pattern using the starting point of Aberdeen and the final destination of Brisbane using the hub airports of Amsterdam Schiphol and Singapore Changi.

- **Instrument Landing System** – More commonly referred to as 'ILS' this is a system which uses ground beacons (localizers) to guide an aircraft down a glide slope and to the runway threshold in extremely low or even zero visibility. The system is categorised from CAT I which requires a certain level of visibility before decision height is reached to CAT III where the aircraft can land in zero visibility conditions. The use of ILS will slowly be replaced with the use of more sophisticated Global Position Systems which will allow even greater precision
- **Long Haul Operations** – The term used for flights which cover great distances. The exact definition of long haul varies with author and organisation. IATA believes that a long haul flight is one which travels between traffic conference areas (see definitions).
- **Point to Point Traffic** – Route network developed around just one set of city pairings. As an example a flight will leave London Stansted bound for Stockholm Arlanda. On arrival, the aircraft will be turned around to return to its original destination Stansted. This method of operation is favoured by Low Cost carriers who are able to gain greater fleet and crew utilisation as a result of this process.
- **Runway** – The strip of tarmac used by aircraft to reach their required speed to enter the flight stage of the journey and then to return the craft to the ground and allow deceleration to occur.

- **Short Haul Operations** – As with long haul, the definition varies based on organisation. IATA have defined short haul as any flight operated within a Traffic Conference Area.
- **Slot** – The time allocated to a flight for either takeoff or landing. At highly congested airports, the failure of an aircraft to meet its slot requirements could mean that the aircraft is delayed for several hours until a new slot can be approved.
- **Stack** – The flow management system used to control aircraft waiting to land at busy airports. Aircraft will enter the stack and will gradually circle around a radio beacon whilst slowly loosing height. This procedure will continue until the slot time arrives when the aircraft will break away from the stack and establish itself on the glideslope for landing. At severely congested airports such as London Heathrow there can be as many as three stacks in operation at any one time.
- **Standard Terminal Arrival Route (STAR)** – A procedure which directs an aircraft from the top of descent and onto the required runway's glideslope. The procedure will involve flying between a number of waypoints (radio beacons) which will require aircraft to turn and descend so as to allow them to reach the required runway at the correct heading and altitude.
- **Standard Instrument Departure (SID)** - A set of flight procedures followed by an aircraft which will allow it to join its required airway. Major international airports will operate a number of SID's depending on the destination of the flight and to reduce noise disturbance to local residents. As with STAR's, a SID is flown using waypoints as a method of controlling direction, speed and height.
- **Taxiway** – The linchpin between the runway and the terminal building. Taxiways are built at an acute angle to the runway so as to allow aircraft to exit quickly and thus increasing the flow of flights from the facility. At certain airports, taxiways may also be used as emergency runways when the main facility is inoperable as is the case at London's Gatwick airport.
- **Terminal** – A building designed for the interconnection of one transport mode and another. In the case of an airport, the terminal acts as the interface between ground and air transportation and the processes required to allow passengers to board their plane (including check in and security procedures). Major hub airports will also act as the connection point between flights allowing passengers to reach their final destination.
- **Traffic Conference Area** – Developed by IATA, the traffic conference area is an administrative breakdown of the world into three distinct regions. Traffic Conference Area 1 (TCA 1) is based on the Americas and includes – North, Latin and South America. Traffic Conference Area 2 encompasses Europe, Middle East and Africa. The final traffic Conference Area 3, houses Asia and the Pacific regions. Within each traffic conference area, there are further breakdowns into regions.
- **Turnaround** – The process of preparing an aircraft for its next flight. The procedure will normally involve refuelling the aircraft, uploading new catering supplies, cleaning the aircraft, loading and unloading passengers and baggage as well as carrying out any essential maintenance work. The length of turnaround varies tremendously between types of operator with Low Cost airlines such as Ryanair looking to complete the procedure in less than 25 minutes. This is highly efficient compared to charter carriers who look to turnaround within 45 minutes and certain scheduled carriers who can take longer than 1 hour.

- **Waypoint** – a named location based on longitudinal and latitudinal coordinates which marks a specific point. Waypoints are often based on radio beacons (non Directional Beacons - NDB's) and help pilots navigate to their desired destination via airways.

Aviation Economic Terminology

- **Available Seat Kilometre** - ASK is the measurement of capacity available and is calculated by multiplying the available number of seats by the distance flown.
- **Demand Elasticity** – Text books often refer to business travellers being 'inelastic' in demand and leisure travellers being 'elastic', but what does this mean? Put simply, business travellers are 'inelastic' in demand due to the fact that as prices increase the level of tickets booked does not go down proportionately. So, a 10% increase in the cost of the ticket may only reduce demand by 1%, often even less. By contrast leisure traveller is termed 'elastic' as when prices increase there will be a proportional reduction in the number of travellers. Equally a decrease in fares helps to stimulate demand.
- **Load Factor** – By dividing RPK's and ASK's, a percentage figure will be arrived at which indicates how full a flight is. Scheduled flights are currently (May 2015) tending to operate at 75 – 79% load factors, but with oil increases and less consumer spending, load factors can drop if capacity is not reigned in.

Task 5

Find and compare the load factors for British Airways (or any other traditional carrier) and that of easyJet (or any other low cost carrier). What do these figures tell you about current market conditions?

- **Revenue Passenger Kilometre** – RPK is the measure of demand based on how many passengers are flown multiplied by the distance travelled
- **Yield** – The average fare paid by a customer calculated on how much each passenger on a flight paid divided by the flights mileage.

- **Yield Management** - A complicated algorithm which attempts to match capacity with demand. By doing so, the price of a ticket will increase as demand for a flight increases but falls where demand is weak allowing airlines to gain maximum revenue based on market conditions.

Key Texts and Journals

Calder, S. (2008) No Frills – The Truth Behind The Low-Cost Revolution In The Skies, 3rd Ed, Virgin Books.

Doganis, R. (2010) Flying Off Course – The Economics of International Airlines, 4th Ed, Amazon Kindle Edition.

Doganis, R. (2005) The Airline Business in the 21st Century, 2nd Ed, Routledge.

Doganis, R. (2002) The Airport Business, Routledge.

Graham, A. (2008) Managing Airports – An International Perspective, 3rd Ed, Butterworth-Heinemann.

Hanlon, P. (2006) Global Airlines, 3rd Ed, Butterworth-Heinemann.

Holloway, J.C. (2006) The Business of Tourism, Seventh Edition, Prentice Hall.

Page, S. (2009) Transport and Tourism, 3rd Ed, Longman.

Pender, L. (2001) Travel Trade and Transport – An Introduction, Continuum.

Wensveen, J. (2015) Air Transportation: A Management Perspective, 8th Ed, Ashgate Publishing.

Journals

Airline Business

Flight International

Journal of Air Transport Management

Tourism management

Travel Trade Gazette

Databases

Keynotes

Mintel International

OAG World Airways Guide

OAG World Travel Atlas

Office of National Statistics – International Passenger Survey (IPS)

Websites

Airlines

British Airways – www.ba.com

British Airways Investor Site – www.bashares.com

British European – www.flybe.com

easyJet – www.easyjet.com

Ryanair – www.ryanair.com

Virgin Atlantic Airways – www.virgin-atlantic.com

Airports

Heathrow Airport – heathrowairport.com

Birmingham Airport – www.bhx.co.uk

JFK New York – www.jfkairport.com

Luton Airport – www.london-luton.com

Manchester Airport – www.manairport.co.uk

Aircraft Manufacturers

Airbus Industries – www.airbus.com

Boeing – www.boeing.com

Alliance Groups

Oneworld – www.oneworldalliance.com

Skyteam – www.skyteam.com

Star Alliance – www.star-alliance.com

Aviation & Government Organisations

Air Transport Action Group - www.atag.org

Department of Transport White Paper - www.dft.gov.uk/aviation/whitepaper

European Union Website – www.europa.eu.int

International Air Transport Association – www.iata.org

International Civil Aviation Organisation – www.icao.org

The Civil Aviation Authority – www.caa.co.uk

Academic Websites

Transport Studies Group – www.wmin.ac.uk/transport

University of Cranfield – www.cranfield.ac.uk

Unit Two

Commercial Aviation – Historical Overview

Unit Objectives:
On completing this unit, you should be able to:

- Demonstrate historical knowledge of the development of commercial aviation
- Identify the main periods of development and the technological advances made
- Examine current commercial aviation issues based on historical knowledge

The History of Commercial Aviation

Mankind's quest for flight has seen him at his most brilliant and at times his most desperate. The fascination with flight dates back to the very earliest of civilisations. From the 6th century, the Chinese used kites to suspend people and an investigation further back to Greek mythology tells of Daedalus and Icarus who created wings out of feathers and tar. Unfortunately, Icarus flew to close to the sun, the tar melted and he plunged from the sky. To fully understand how we have finally achieved mechanical flight, it is best to break the historical developments down into the following periods, namely:

- The dream of flight
- The revolutionary period
- The military advantage
- Heroic challenges
- The battle for the skies
- The Passenger Jet
- The Computer Age
- Present and future developments

The dream of flight

Many intrepid inventors have perished trying to be the first to experience flight and the feeling of freedom associated with the heavens. From jumping off towers with wing like structures, to cycling along beaches at breakneck speeds, many have tried to overcome gravity and enter the atmosphere.

The first successful flights can be traced back to the 2nd century when gliders were used to travel over very short distances. While these in themselves were fantastic achievements, most people think of the foremost intellectual within the area of flight as being Leonardo da Vinci. Even though he never achieved flight himself due to the lack of light weight materials and a sustainable power supply, his 1487 design for the 'Ornithopter' appears in most texts as being the first design for an aircraft, even though the concept was totally impracticable.

It was not until 1670 when an inventor by the name of Francesco de Lana realised that one of the easiest ways of achieving flight was to create a machine which was lighter than air. Whilst, he may have realised this it was not until 1783 that the first manned balloon flight took place when the Montgolfier brothers undertook a flight in Paris to roughly 6,500 feet, although not with them aboard. The only issue with the flight was that the wood fire that produced the hot air to lift the balloon soon engulfed the craft and the passengers were quickly brought back to the ground. These first balloons suffered due to the lack of steering ability but slowly this was rectified.

The revolutionary period

In 1853 Sir George Cayley produced the first controllable glider and through his knowledge of physics introduced the terms 'lift' and 'drag' to the aeronautical world. By 1889, Otto Lilenthal had furthered the research into flight and produced a book looking at aerodynamic theory. His passion for flight ultimately caused his death as he fell whilst trying to add to his 2,500 attempts to fly using glider technology. The pace of invention did not cease within this period. Famous pioneers included Percy Pilcher who lost his life in 1899 to one of his flying inventions and Edward Frost who in 1902 produced a flapping wing machine. Remnants of Frost's flapping wing machine are to be found at the British Museum and are indelibly etched on the conscience of anyone who has seen the film The Magnificent Men in their Flying Machines.

Just one year after Frost's attempt to become airborne, two brothers on a beach near Kitty Hawk, North Carolina achieved the impossible, as the Wright brothers Flyer took to the air for a distance of 121 feet in a time of 12 seconds. To achieve this flight, they used all the mechanical know how that they had developed as bike mechanics and took a keen interest in the publication of Otto Lilenthal.

Information: *The Wright brothers' first flight would not have reached from one end of economy class to the other on a Boeing 747 'Jumbo Jet'!!*

The discovery by the Wright brothers soon spread across the globe and it was not long before new versions of the Wright Flyer were being produced and improved. The first European 'heavier-than-air' flight took place in Paris in 1906. In 1909, Louis Bleriot won the Daily Mail challenge to fly across the English Channel in a respectable time of 37 minutes.

The military advantage

At the start of the First World War, aircraft technology remained at best rudimentary. This did not however stop their use for military conflict. Initially, their role was as reconnaissance aircraft but it soon became apparent that they could also be used as fighting weapons in their own right. Aircraft were soon involved in air to air combat with legends being created around the adventures of pilots such Manfred Von Richthofen or, as he became known, the 'Red Baron'. As the conflict developed the design and materials used to build aircraft changed. As production techniques improved so did aircraft reliability. The ability to carry increased weight allowed aircraft to carry heavier bomb loads which made such methods a real possibility for the first time even though aerial bombardment by airship had been banned under the 1899 Hague Convention.

At the end of the First World War, it soon became apparent that the use of aircraft could serve a civilian role as well. Initially, such services were based on airmail but it was not long before the concept of commercial passenger flights was put forward. The first daily international scheduled passenger air service was launched in August 1919 between Hounslow (not far from the present Heathrow Airport) and Le Bourget near Paris. For £42, passengers endured a three hour flight which was not guaranteed especially during bad weather. The first flight was perhaps not so successful with its full payload being two passengers the aircraft took off with a 50% load factor, i.e. one passenger!

The development of the commercial airline industry was rapid. Airline companies were created including Deutsche Luft Reederei (the forerunner of Lufthansa), Imperial Airways (after a number of reincarnations including BOAC - British Airways) and KLM – Royal Dutch Airlines (created in 1919 and the world's oldest scheduled airline to keep the same name - Koninklijke Luchtvaart Maatschappij). These airlines used second-hand military aircraft to ply routes across the globe with passengers experiencing at best, Spartan conditions. These conditions did improve over time however, and by 1925 Deutsche Luft Hansa was showing films on board its flights.

Whilst aircraft were being developed for commercial services during the 1920's, airships were streets ahead in terms of comfort and distance. The development in 1928 of the Graf Zeppelin signified the high point in airship services. During 1929 the Graf Zeplin undertook a round the world trip but was mostly employed on scheduled services operating from Europe to the East Coast of the United States. Zeppelins operated for ten years before the loss of the Hindenburg in New Jersey USA, safety concerns and stopped people using them even though most passengers survived the crash.

The airship may have received lots of attention during its brief history but competing with them, and transporting far more passengers, were the flying boats of commercial airlines such as Pan American Airways Systems and Imperial Airways. Routes were flown across the globe with aircraft calling not at landlocked airports but at ports. Flying boats were decked out in the latest styles with accommodation comprising of bunk beds, lounges and a restaurant.

Heroic Challenges

Whilst commercial aviation was progressing at pace, the need to push aircraft and aviators continued unabated by accidents or disaster. In 1927 Charles Lindberg became the first man to fly solo between New York and Paris in the Spirit of St Louis. The success of this voyage has been turned into a feature film and the aircraft still enjoys pride of place at the National Air and Space Museum in Washington D.C. It was not just men who were setting records. In 1928, American Amelia Earhart flew single handed across the Atlantic and in 1930 Amy Johnson undertook the first female solo flight between Britain to Australia.

In 1930, Frank Whittle a Royal Air Force pilot developed the first designs for an aircraft engine with no moving parts. With little encouragement from the British Government, he worked tirelessly on his designs over many years until in 1937 he tested the first prototype jet engine.

As Frank Whittle was working on his ambitious plans for the jet engine, a scientist by the name of Robert Watson-Watt was completing his study into RADAR and by 1935 had perfected his first prototype system. The development of both these technologies came at a time when relations within Europe had reached yet another all time low. In 1939, Europe was once again thrown into war. Commercial air services started to take a back seat as the war effort required all manufacturers to focus on military hardware.

The Battle for the Skies

As with the First World War, the Second World War as with the first brought rapid development of aircraft. This included in 1944 the first jet flight by a Gloster Meteor. It was, however, a military logistics aircraft that was to change the face of civilian passenger air services after the war. The Douglas DC – 3 or 'Dakota' as it was named, proved to be a resilient aircraft which after the war became the backbone of civil airlines across the globe, with most of the aircraft being purchased second hand from US, Canadian and United Kingdom Air Forces. With the aid of these aircraft, governments across the world sat up and realised the importance of civil airlines. In 1948 the Berlin Airlift used civilian aircraft to transport supplies to the then cut off West Berlin. Probably one of the most famous aviators who took part within this operation was Sir Freddie Laker who was later to set up Laker Airways.

Task 1

Investigate how the Berlin Airlift helped develop the UK charter airline industry.

The Passenger Jet

The first commercial flight by passenger jet was in 1949 when the de Havilland Comet made its first maiden flight. By 1952, the Comet was in regular service with British Overseas Airways Corporation (BOAC – the forerunner to British Airways). The first jetliner did not get off to the best of starts and with fatal accidents seeming to happen frequently, the aircraft was soon grounded. The aircraft underwent painstaking investigations to determine what was at fault. The answer it seemed was the window design which created stress cracks which ultimately led to the fuselage being ripped apart.

Task 2

As scheduled airlines tried to gain a competitive advantage by buying 'jetliners' what happened to all their second hand turboprop aircraft?

While de Havilland and the UK air industry was busy trying to solve the Comets problems, Boeing in the United States developed a similar four engine jet aircraft that would take the world by storm – the Boeing 707 was born. Ordered by Juan Trippe the Pan American Airlines boss, the 707 was used on services across the Atlantic from 1958. It was not long before Boeing had competition from the newly designed Comet 4 and the Douglas DC – 8.

The development of passenger jets accelerated for both long haul and short haul markets. The most notable developments included:-

- 1958 – de Havilland Trident 121 & Douglas DC-8

- 1959 – Aerospatiale Caravelle – 1st rear engine aircraft

- 1960 – Avro HS748

- 1961 – Vickers VC-10

- 1963 – BAC 1-11 & Boeing 727

- 1965 – Douglas DC-9

- 1967 – Boeing 737

- 1969 – Boeing 747

KLM Boeing 747 – 400 (*photographed by the author*)

Task 3

Investigate in what ways did the introduction of the Boeing 747 revolutionise air travel?

- 1969 – British Aerospace / Aerospatiale Concorde

The last Concorde landed at London Heathrow on 24th October 2003. All but one of British Airways fleet of these supersonic aircraft have been donated to museums. The only example left at London Heathrow is currently just left outside British Airways maintenance base. (*Photographed by the author*)

Task 4

Highlight the main advantages that a passenger could experience flying on Concorde. Why was the aircraft withdrawn from service by British Airways and Air France in 2003?

- 1970 – Lockheed L1011 Tri-Star & Mc Donnell Douglas DC -10

- 1972 – Airbus A300 – The first two crew cockpit commercial airliner

- 1981 – Boeing 767

- 1982 – Boeing 757

- 1982 – Airbus A310

Task 5

Juan Trippe is one of the most famous airline executives. Investigate his working life and highlight the revolutionary decisions that he made and the affect these have had on commercial aviation. Further information available at http://en.wikipedia.org/wiki/Juan_Trippe

The Computer Age

Although technologically advanced in their own right, as with other areas of modern life, aircraft have developed over the past two decades based on information technology. The first aircraft to embrace the concept of computer control was the Airbus A320 which was the first aircraft to deliver commands to its control surfaces not by wires and hydraulics but by computer messages. The cockpit of these new airliners was also very different from what had gone before; anyone who has glanced into the cockpit of this new generation of jets will be faced not with dials and switches but with colour LCD screens and computer keyboards. The flight control on airbus aircraft was also revolutionised by no longer having a flight yoke set in front of the pilot but by having a small hand operated joystick placed next to them. The main computer age developments are listed below:-

- 1984 – Airbus Industries launches the first 'fly-by-wire' aircraft the A320 (flies in 1987) & Boeing 737-300 first flight.

- 1988 – Boeing 747-400 takes to the air

- 1991 – First maiden flight for both the A330 & A340

- 1993 – First A321 flight

- 1994 – Boeing 777 maiden flight

- 1995 – First A319 flight

- 1996 – Boeing launch the first Next Generation 737

Present and future developments

The later part of the 1990's and the beginning of the 21st Century have seen the two biggest aircraft manufacturers disagreeing as to how the future market for airliners will look. Boeing believes that current and future passengers are looking for point-to-point route networks which allow them to bypass major hub airports thus helping reduce the stress of flight. To this end, Boeing has developed the highly sophisticated long range ultra comfortable Boeing 787 jetliner. On the other hand, Airbus has targeted Boeing's past stronghold, namely the Boeing 747. Airbus believes that the only way airlines will be able to cope with congested airways and hubs is to build bigger aircraft which again offer the most comfortable passenger experience. Airbus has therefore created the A380 double decker long range 'super jumbo'. The success of this decision so far seems to be in Boeing's corner as Airbus failed to sell even one A380 in 2014 and its future has been called into question by a variety of aviation commentators.

One of the few areas that both companies have agreed upon is the need for future aircraft to be far more environmentally friendly. Both the Boeing 787 and Airbus A350/A380 use the latest light weight but extremely strong composite material while at the same time employ far more fuel efficient and environmentally friendly power plants which have helped to reduce fuel consumption and noise.

Task 6

Outline the main technologies that have been introduced by the 787 and A350/A380 aimed at helping improve commercial aviation's environmental credentials.

Future developments are still difficult to predict as aircraft technology progresses rapidly. Organisations such as NASA believe that one day individual aircraft will be operating just as cars are today. Others point to the need to develop hypersonic transport which would use a mixture of rocket propulsion and jet engines to blast passengers from London to Sydney in less than three hours. Whatever developments do occur the need for environmental sustainability will probably drive the next generation of jets as residents, passengers and governments look to tackle global warming and airlines look to reduce their fuel bills.

Aviation Legislation – Historical Timeline

Date	Event
1919	Paris Air Navigation Convention
1929	Warsaw Convention
1944	Chicago Convention – Establishment of ICAO
1946	Bermuda Bilateral Agreement – US & UK
1955	The Hague Protocol
1971	Guatemala City Protocol – further amendments to Hague Protocol
1977	Bermuda II Bilateral Agreement – US & UK
1978	US Deregulation
1987	European Union - First Package for Air Deregulation – intra – European flights
1990	European Union – Second Package for Air Deregulation – Greater freedom on fares and capacity
1993	European Union – Third Package for Air Deregulation – Cabotage Rights introduced (from 1997)
1999	Montreal Convention
2004	EU Denied-boarding Compensation Scheme
2008	US – EU Open Skies Agreement

Further detail concerning aviation law and legislation can be found under sections nine and ten of this text.

Conclusion

The aim of this unit has been to highlight the historical influences upon commercial aviation. The history of commercial aviation is very short, less than 100 years old, but its advancements have been meteoric. The next remaining units will look at how airlines, airports and aircraft manufacturers are looking to progress these developments.

References and Suggested Further Reading

Grant, R.G. (2002) Flight – 100 Years of Aviation, Dorking Kindersley.

Heppenheimer, T. (1995) Turbulent Skies: History of Commercial Aviation, John Wiley and Son.

Rhoades, D.L. (2003) Evolution of International Aviation: Phoenix Rising, Ashgate Publishing.

Visit http://www.bamuseum.com/index.html to find out details of visiting the British Airways Museum at London Heathrow.

Unit Three

The Airline Industry

Unit Objectives:

On completing this unit, you should be able to:

- Identify the different types of air carrier
- Understand the importance of commercial aviation to the global economy
- Distinguish between traditional scheduled carriers and charter airlines
- Comprehend the development of low cost carriers
- Understand the differences between cargo and integrated carriers

Introduction

Within this unit we are going to look at the definition and differences between the types of airline that serve the United Kingdom and Europe. The European Union (2014) has estimated that there are over 387 airlines within Europe. Globally, Holloway (2006) estimated that there are over 650 scheduled airlines.

The Airline Industry

The airline industry is often split into three main types of operator:

1. Traditional Scheduled or Full Service Network Carrier– including British Airways, Virgin Atlantic and American Airlines
2. Traditional Charter Carriers – including Thomas Cook Airlines and Monarch
3. Low Cost Carriers – including Ryanair, easyJet and Air Berlin

Apart from these operators, Holloway (2006) also highlights the role of Air Taxi Services (although these are more commonly called Business Jets within aviation). A further two categories of airline are illustrated by Wensveen (2015) in the form of all cargo airlines (including Gemini Air Cargo or Polar Air Cargo) and Integrated carriers (such as Fed Ex and United Parcel Service). For this particular text, we will just concentrate on the three main sectors of traditional scheduled, charter and low cost carriers. Table 3.1 highlights the scheduled airlines operating in the UK during 2014.

Table 3.1 – UK Scheduled Airlines Passenger Carryings for 2014

Airline	Passengers Carried	Notes
AURIGNY AIR SERVICES	518878	
BA CITYFLYER LTD	1612947	LCY Operations apart from JFK
BLUE ISLANDS LIMITED	332635	
BMI REGIONAL	309756	
BRITISH AIRWAYS (BA) LTD	23836	LCY - JFK A318 Operation
BRITISH AIRWAYS PLC	39527941	LHR / LGW Mainline Operations
EASTERN AIRWAYS	288450	
EASYJET AIRLINE COMPANY LTD	54137361	
FLYBE LTD	7108588	
ISLES OF SCILLY SKYBUS	89189	
JET2.COM LTD	5931230	
LOGANAIR	640987	
MONARCH AIRLINES	6269624	
THOMAS COOK AIRLINES LTD	1684890	
THOMSON AIRWAYS LTD	369946	
VIRGIN ATLANTIC AIRWAYS LTD	5963367	

Source: CAA (2015)

http://www.caa.co.uk/docs/80/airline_data/2014Annual/Table_0_1_7_1_All_Scheduled_Services_2014.pdf

Traditional Scheduled or Network Carrier

Traditional scheduled airlines tend to be defined on the fact that they operate to a fixed timetable. Holloway (2006) highlights that scheduled airlines "operate on defined routes, domestic or international, for which licences have been granted by the governments concerned. The airlines are required to operate on the basis of their published timetable, regardless of passenger load factors." It was common practice for scheduled airlines to be owned by the government and operate as a symbol of the nation; hence carriers such as British Airways are still often referred to as 'National Flag Carriers'. This situation changed in the 1980's, however, as the aviation industry entered a period of deregulation. Soon governments started to realise the potential savings that could be made by turning monolithic cost burdens that ate into taxpayer's revenue into public companies, which would need to fend for themselves. British Airways was one of the first flag carriers to meet this fate in 1987 having been turned around from a heavy loss making institution into a lean and fit airline that for once could live up-to its then advertising slogan as the 'world's favourite airline'.

Few airlines remain in state control. In Europe, the practice has been ruled out by European Union competition rules, although many airlines still have state influence or minority shareholdings. However, this has not stopped two of the most inefficient carriers, Alitalia and Olympic Airways, from still sheltering under their respective governments wings. Alitalia has been thrown a lifeline by Etihad of Abu Dhabi who have acquired a 49% shareholding in the company. The European airline scene is still fraught for most players with brand names including Malev (2012) and Cyprus Airways

(2014) going into receivership and LOT Polish Airlines having been given its final tranche of state aid following intervention by the European Union.

Most traditional scheduled airlines tend to operate around a 'hub and spoke' network (see definitions in Unit One) that allows them to gain greater efficiency and at the same time serve a larger number of destinations. Scheduled carriers have witnessed massive change over the past decade on two fronts which has caused some of them to reconsider using hubbing. The main attacks have tended to come from the Low Cost Carriers who have taken a fair share of the traditional network carrier's short and domestic business. This has made some regional routes less economic to run, thereby reducing the spokes available. The growth of Middle Eastern carriers, such as Emirates, Qatar and Etihad Airways, has had major implications for carriers such as British Airways, Qantas and Singapore Airlines. The Middle Eastern carriers entice passengers to fly via cities such as Dubai to Australia and Asia from the UK with lower fares and higher service standards together with new state of the art airports which are specifically designed to handle transit passengers on offer.

To counter such threats, carriers including British Airways have formed airline alliances which have helped boost the number of destinations they serve and increase their marketing power. The three main airline alliances are currently Star, Oneworld and Skyteam.

Task 1

Look at the following websites and list which airlines belong to the following airline alliances:

www.oneworld.com	www.skyteam.com	www.staralliance.com

Task 2

List three UK traditional carriers and investigate what type of route network they operate.

The deregulation of air space and privatisation of previously state controlled airlines has helped stimulate competition across the European Union. Whilst both passengers and airports welcome this competition it has led to instability and financial insecurity for many traditional airlines operating in Europe. It has already been noted that a number of airlines, most of whom were in the past owned by national governments have gone bankrupt. Examples include, Swissair, Sabena and more recently Cyprus Airways. To counter the threat of competition, especially from low cost carriers, and help increase market power, the larger airlines found within Europe have initiated a strategy of consolidation. This simply involves airlines such as Lufthansa acquiring smaller carriers within European markets that its business strategy dictates it should have a presence. The acquisition of established airlines is strategically safer than growing a market organically. Figure 3.1 identifies the three main airline groups found in Europe.

Fig 3.1 - European Airline Groups

Lufthansa Group	Air France/ KLM Group	International Airlines Group
Lufthansa	Air France	British Airways
Air Dolomiti	Brit Air	British Airways City Flyer
Lufthansa Regional	Air France Hop	Iberia
Austrian Airlines	KLM	Iberia Express
Swiss	KLM City Hopper	Air Nostrum
Eurowings	Martinair	Openskies
Germanwings	Transavia.com (NL & FR)	Vuelling
Sun Express (50%)		Sun-Air
Ukraine Airlines (22%)		Air Nostrum
STAR ALLIANCE	**SKYTEAM ALLIANCE**	**Oneworld**

Source: Airline websites (May 2015)

Charter Airlines

Charter airlines operate by hiring out their services to third parties such as tour operators who then use these aircraft as a means of producing their product, in this case a package holiday. As charter carriers operate to the demands of the hirer there tends not to be a fix timetable in the same sense as for scheduled operators. This is not to say that the charter carrier will not operate to a timetable for a fixed season e.g. summer or winter holiday seasons.

The importance of charter airlines to the tour operating industry is best illustrated by the fact the most UK charter carriers are owned outright by their tour operating parent – a process called 'vertical integration' an illustration of this is shown in table 3.2.

Table 3.2 – UK Tour Operating Company Ownership

Tour Operator	Charter Airline	Other Business Interest
Thomson	Thomson Airways	Travel agencies, cruise-ships and hotel operations
Thomas Cook	Thomas Cook Airlines	Travel agencies

The type of charter contract can be broken down into the following forms:

1. **Time-series charter** – *an aircraft is taken for a set period of time often by one large tour operator. The time period is often one season at a time.*
2. **Part Charters** – *used where one tour operator is unable to afford or sell the whole of an aircraft for a particular route. Part charters can be a 50/50 split or based on smaller percentages based on the number of tour operators looking to serve the route.*
3. **Ad hoc Charters** – *an 'as and where' service. Aircraft are made available on a 24-hour basis to cover maintenance issues with other aircraft or to offer new services at short notice.*

The scale of charter airline operations within Europe has reduced dramatically over the last decade. In 2014 one of the oldest charter airlines, Monarch, went through a turbulent buyout process that has resulted in the airline withdrawing from the charter airline market completely. The future of even the largest charter airline group - TUI AG is uncertain as the company looks to consolidate around one core brand. At the time of writing the future of Thomas Cook Airlines had also been called into question and awaits the decision of its board as to its strategic direction.

Task 3

Investigate the different types of service a passenger could expect to experience based on scheduled and charter carrier operations. What main target markets are attracted to scheduled and charter services? How do these target markets affect the product offered?

Low Cost Carriers

Although Low Cost Carriers, or New Model Airlines as they are sometimes referred to operate along the same lines as scheduled airlines i.e. operate to a fixed published timetable, they do operate a very different business model to traditional scheduled airlines. They can best be defined as an airline which offers low fares by constantly reducing and monitoring their cost base. Figure 3.1 illustrates the generic business model which is followed by the majority of low cost operators across the globe.

Figure 3.1 – Low Cost Airlines Virtuous Circle Business Model

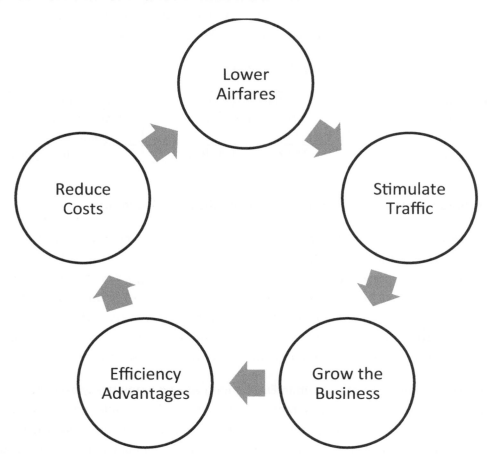

Low cost airlines owe their existence to the deregulation and liberalisation of air services initially within the United States of America (which created carriers such as People Express and ValuJet) and then in the mid 1990's the EU Third Package of Air Transport Liberalisation saw the birth of easyJet and Ryanair.

There are some major differences between traditional scheduled carriers and Low Cost operators. The main differences between these operators are summarised in the table 3.3.

Table 3.3 – Different operating characteristics between Low Cost Carriers and Scheduled Airlines

Low Cost Carrier	Traditional Scheduled Carrier
Basic and easily recognisable brand	Sophisticated brand which highlights companies benefits. Brand segmented to attract different markets
Point-to-point itineraries only with no connections available	Complex hub operations with high level of interconnections and interlining
Simplified fare structure – based on lowest fare, length before departure date and demand.	Complex fare structure based on different classes of service available. Yield management has allowed carriers to be as competitive as low cost operations.
No in-flight service unless you pay for items	Long haul operations still offer full service. Economy class service on Europe routes has changed to compete with low cost carriers, e.g. SAS charges for in-flight food and alcoholic drinks in economy class but has become more competitive with Low Cost operators based on cost.
Mostly operate from 'secondary' and 'tertiary' airports	Operate from major hub airports located close to city areas.
Operate primarily on short haul routes – allow greater utilisation of aircraft	Mixed route structure with domestic and short haul flights feeding into intercontinental services
Common fleet type which allows for reduction in training and maintenance costs	Mix of aircraft used due to variety of routes served
Outsourcing and employee productivity increases based on ownership scheme and broader job descriptions	Highly unionised work force that have specific job roles. Level of outsourcing is increasing as cost reductions are sought
Standardised cabin with no seat allocation	Mixed cabin configuration depending on route with each seat pre assigned before take off
Sales through internet (Ryanair currently at 98%)	Mixed sales distribution currently but carriers such as British Airways looking to move above 85% bookings from internet

The spread of Low Cost Airlines has been rapid with them today being found on each continent. The list below features the main carriers involved in the low cost operations across the globe.

Can you think of any others?

North America & Canada

Europe

Asia Pacific

Africa & Middle East

Latin & South America

Task 4

The difference between fares offered by Low Cost Carrier versus Traditional Scheduled Airlines is a favourite topic of Sunday newspaper travel sections. For this task you are asked to choose ONE European city that has both a low cost and traditional scheduled airline flying to it. On choosing a destination you are then asked to compare the price found on their website for a flight which leaves at roughly the same time of day for the following notice periods:-

	Low Cost Carrier Price (£)	Traditional Scheduled Airline Price (£)
Next Day		
2 Weeks notice		
2 Months notice		
6 months notice		

1. Are there any big differences in the price charged? Why do you believe this is the case?

2. Can you identify from your research when a scheduled carrier may be cheaper than the low cost operators?

3. Do Low Cost Airline tickets reflect the true cost of travel compared to scheduled operators?

Air Cargo

The carriage of cargo is undertaken by three distinct types of operator, which are highlighted below:-

1.   Schedule Airline Cargo Operations
2.   Dedicated cargo carrier
3.   Integrated Carrier

Schedule Airline Cargo Operations

Most traditional scheduled airlines help cover the cost of their services by carrying cargo on the bottom deck or 'belly hold' of passenger aircraft. Some airlines employ what are termed 'combi' aircraft that allow carriers to carry cargo and passengers on the main deck as well as using the belly hold for additional cargo. This tends to be a profitable venture when there is not as strong demand for passenger services on a route compared to cargo traffic.

Airlines including Lufthansa have also introduced what are termed quick conversion 'QC' aircraft which allow them the carry passengers by day but then to quickly remove the seats at night from the main deck so as to fill it with freight.

Dedicated Cargo Airline

Dedicated cargo airlines are airlines that specialise in the carriage of freight. Some may be owned and operated jointly by traditional scheduled airlines. This category includes Lufthansa Cargo and Air France Cargo. There are also specific cargo operators that specialise in the movement of freight, for example Atlas Air Cargo, Cargolux, and Volga-Dnepr.

The aircraft used by dedicated cargo airlines are normally hybrid versions of commercial passenger aircraft including the Boeing 747, 777 and Airbus A300. The only modifications that are made to allow the movement of cargo include a larger door (which on the Boeing 747 incorporates the nose opening upwards to allow cargo to enter) and strengthened wings and fuselage to take the extra weight.

Integrated Carrier

Integrated carriers are companies that transport freight door-to-door. Examples of these type of carrier include United Parcel Service (UPS), Federal Express (FedEx), TNT and DHL. These companies have developed sophisticated information technology logistic systems that allow both sender and recipients to track the progress of their package. Their contribution to commercial aviation is often overlooked. For example, it was Federal Express who first developed and practiced the concept of hub-and-spoke operations.

Task 5

Return to table 3.1 that highlights the scheduled airlines operating in the UK. For this task you are asked to visit each of the carrier's respective websites and find out the required information to complete the table below:

Airline	Route Structure Long / Short Haul	Main Hub Airport (s)	Number of Aircraft & Type	Type of Operation
BA CITYFLYER LTD				
BMI REGIONAL				
BRITISH AIRWAYS				
EASYJET				
FLYBE LTD				
JET2.COM LTD				
MONARCH AIRLINES				
THOMAS COOK AIRLINES LTD				
THOMSON AIRWAYS				
VIRGIN ATLANTIC AIRWAYS				

Why are not all the airlines in table 3.1 represented above – which ones are missing and why?

Conclusions

Within this unit we have investigated the different types of air carrier operating within the UK and around the globe. The development of low cost airlines has been rapid and of huge benefit to leisure travellers looking to explore new parts of Europe. However, this development may be soon curtailed as environmental and oil price pressures mount. The next unit will look at how airports operate as a business and look to attract low cost airlines as well as other carriers to operate from their facilities.

References and Suggested Further Reading

CAA (2015) www.caa.co.uk

European Union (2007) Flying Together: EU air transport policy, Office for Official Publications of the European Communities, Luxembourg.

Hewson, R. & Endres, G.G (2003) The Vital Guide to Major Airlines of the World, The Crowood Press Ltd.

Holloway, J.C. (2006) The Business of Tourism, Numerous Editions, Longman.

Oxford Economic Forecasting (2006) The Economic Contribution of the Aviation Industry in the UK http://www.oef.com/Free/pdfs/Aviation2006Final.pdf

Wensveen, J. (2015) Air Transportation: A Management Perspective; 8th Ed, Ashgate Publishing.

Unit Four

The Airport Business

Unit Objectives:
On completing this unit, you should be able to:

- Identify the different ownership structures of airports
- Explain the types of airport used for commercial aviation purposes
- Distinguish between the size categories of airports throughout the UK
- Identify the main growth opportunities available to regional and local airports

Introduction

Airports act as the interchange that allows passengers to transfer between modes of transport either to start or finish their air travel or simply to transfer from one flight to another. Before we begin this unit it is probably wise to distinguish between the term airport and airfield. An airport has been defined by the UK Civil Aviation Authority (CAA) as any facility dominated by commercial aviation operations. Lober (2004) in his report General Aviation Small Aerodrome Research Study (GASAR) defines an airfield as a facility which undertakes General Aviation operations.

The airport business is in essence a simple one – offer landing and take off slots to airlines and the facilities required to process passengers. However, airports make money from both airlines and passengers. An airport looks to gain financial reward from airlines by charging for landing, parking and take off slots plus the use of facilities within the airport such as air bridges and check-in facilities. Airports generate revenue from passengers by offering retail services within the waiting lounges and charging for car parking and other services that it offers directly to the customer.

Within this unit we will concentrate on the following areas of the airport business:

- Airport Ownership
- Types of Airport
- Airport Size

Airport Ownership

The ownership of airports varies around the world with a number owned by governments at national, regional or local level; others are privately operated with a further tranche run via public/private sector partnerships. Within the United Kingdom and Europe, airports are run by a mix of public and private sector organisations. In the UK for example, the British Airports Authority (BAA) was privatised under the Airports Act of 1986. In 2006, the group was purchased by a consortium led by the Spanish infrastructure conglomerate Ferrovial for £10 billion. BAA which once had a monopoly on London Airports controlling London Heathrow, Gatwick and Stansted airports, has seen this situation change due to a Monopolies and Mergers Commission inquiry. Today BAA consists of just Heathrow Airport and as such the group was renamed in 2012 to Heathrow Airport Holdings Ltd (HAH) to take this into account. Table 4.1 highlights the ownership of the main UK commercial airports.

Table 4.1 – UK Airport Ownership

Airport	Ownership
Belfast City – George Best	ABN Amro
Belfast International	Airports Worldwide
Birmingham	Seven district councils own 49% and a further 48% owned by Airport Group Investments Ltd
Bournemouth	Manchester Airport Group – Owned by 10 local authorities around Manchester including Greater Manchester which has a 55% stake in the group.
Bristol	Ontario Teachers' Pension Plan
Cardiff	Welsh Government (100%)
Coventry	Patriot Aviation Group
Durham Tees Valley	Peel Investments Group (89%) & 5 local authorities (11%)
East Midlands	Manchester Airport Group – Owned by 10 local authorities around Manchester including Greater Manchester which has a 55% stake in the group.
Edinburgh	Global Infrastructure Partners (GIP)
Exeter	Rigby Group PLC
Glasgow	AGS Airports
Humberside	Manchester Airport Group – Owned by 10 local authorities around Manchester including Greater Manchester that has a 55% stake in the group.
Leeds Bradford	Bridgepoint Capital – but three local authorities hold special share to make sure of its continued commercial success.
Liverpool	Peel Group
London City Airport	HighStar Capital (25%) and Global Infrastructure Partners – GIP (75%).
London Gatwick	Global Infrastructure Partners (GIP) hold a 41% stake with various other minority holdings.
London Heathrow	Heathrow Airport Holdings, which includes Ferrovial (25%)
London Luton	Luton Borough Council
London Stansted	Manchester Airport Group
Manchester	Manchester Airport Group – Owned by 10 local authorities around Manchester including Greater Manchester which has a 55% stake in the group.
Newcastle	Seven local authorities (51%) & AMP Capital (49%)
Norwich	Omniport (80.1%) & two local authorities (19.9%)
Robin Hood Doncaster	Peel Group
Southampton	AGS Airports

Researched at the individual airports websites (May 2015)

Task 1

Look at table 4.1 and discuss the different ownership patterns found within UK airports.

Interestingly, within the United States either national or regional government owns airports, which is in sharp contrast to the airline sector that has always remained outside the public sector. Airports operate under the auspices of Local Port Authorities, for example, New York's airports JKK, Newark and La Guardia are operated by the Port Authority of New York and New Jersey.

Types of Airport and Size

Airports are broken down into three main types, namely 'Hub' airports, 'Regional' airports and 'Local' airports. Hub airports are located in large cities and act as a transfer point as well as the starting and end point for travellers (often termed international gateways). London Heathrow is a classic example of a hub airport as it serves 185 destinations across the world by a total of 80 airlines, with over 36% of, passengers (26.3 million out of 73.4 million – 2014) transferring at the airport from one flight to another (HAH, 2014). London Heathrow is British Airways and Virgin Atlantic's primary hub airport; both carriers also operate a secondary 'leisure market' hub at London Gatwick Airport. Airlines have tried to use their influence at hub airports to stop competition from entering the market; these are referred to as 'fortress hubs' and are predominately found within the United States of America.

Hub airports are currently experiencing a number of difficulties most of which have been caused by the growing volumes of air travellers. Airports such as London Heathrow have reached the limits of their capacity even with the opening of Terminal Five. The main problem here is the lack of available take off and landing slots due to the airport operating just two runways.

Task 2

Apart from building new runways which will cause environmental damage and residential resentment, what ways can governments act so as to help reduce the strains on major gateway airports such as LHR?

London Heathrow is a major hub airport for both British Airways and Virgin Atlantic (Photographed by author)

Regional and local airports are the second and third category of facility found within commercial aviation. The use of regional and local airports can be broken down into a number of operations, which include:

- **Scheduled services to hub airports for onward connections**

    Within the UK, because of the congested facilities and poor customer experience at London Heathrow, airline customers are starting to use 'feeder' services to Paris (CDG) and Amsterdam (AMS) to connect seamlessly to their onward journey. The popularity of these services is best represented by KLM who currently serve 13 regional airports plus London Heathrow and London City Airport (illustrated in figure 4.1).

    At certain regional airports airlines have looked at bypassing hubs altogether and flying passengers to popular long haul destinations directly. A good example of this practice is Bristol Airport where Continental Airlines offers a daily Boeing 757 departure to New York

Figure 4.1 – KLM UK Route Network

Source: KLM Website (July 2012)

- **Scheduled services to other regional centres**

    The operation of routes between regional airports is fraught with difficulty specifically in a domestic context as passengers often have various other transport modes available to them to reach their destination. The same cannot be said for short haul international flights where low cost airlines have specialised in operating from regional airports across the whole of Europe. For example Ryanair currently has 12 regional hub airports just in the UK (including Bristol, Luton, Stansted, Birmingham, East Midlands, Liverpool, Prestwick and Edinburgh – see figure 4.2).

    Figure 4.2 – Ryanair operates 12 regional hubs from the UK

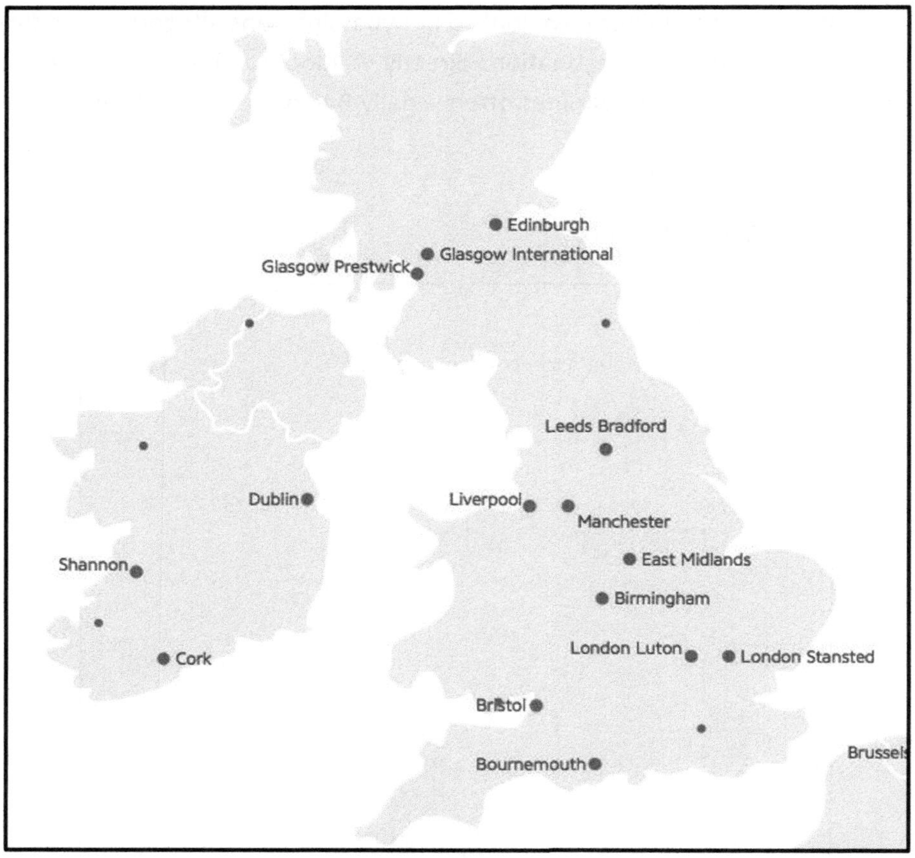

    Source: Ryanair Website (May 2015)

- **Charter services to holiday destinations and sporting events**

    Prior to the arrival of low cost airlines, most UK regional airports tended to generate most of their income from charter flights to holiday destinations across Europe. In the summer, this was based around the Mediterranean (with airports offering longer runways offering flights mostly to Orlando, Florida). In the winter, ski flights to France, Austria and Switzerland were the mainstay plus a few winter sun routes.

Taking into account airport size, it can be seen in table 4.2 that within the UK there is a massive difference between the main London hubs, and airports at Manchester and Birmingham compared to passenger numbers at the rest of the UK's airports. The gap between London Heathrow and the rest of the UK's airports should not be a surprise as Table 4.3 highlights that LHR is the world's third busiest airport. What is of interest is how small airports such as Robin Hood Doncaster Airport look to grow. From their website the Airport Director, Mike Morton, has highlighted that he want the airport to grow based on the following:

"I am determined that we put this airport in a position to always be looking for improved efficiencies in order to be as competitive as possible. At the same time however, looking for greater opportunities, not only in the passenger business where we have made tremendous progress in just three years of operations, but also in the freight market, Business and General Aviation sectors" Mike Morton, Robin Hood Doncaster Website, July 2008.

Task 3

As Managing Director for Cardiff Airport what ways would you look to expand the business based on the information in Table 4.2 and from the relevant information to be found at the airports website: http://info.cwlfly.com/en/content/4/274/masterplan.html and the Department of Transports Website: http://www.dft.gov.uk/about/strategy/whitepapers/air/chapter6wales

Table 4.2 – UK Airport Passenger Numbers 2014

Airport	Total Passengers
HEATHROW	73405330
GATWICK	38103667
MANCHESTER	21989682
STANSTED	19941593
LUTON	10484938
EDINBURGH	10160004
BIRMINGHAM	9705955
GLASGOW	7715988
BRISTOL	6339805
NEWCASTLE	4516739
EAST MIDLANDS INTERNATIONAL	4510544
BELFAST INTERNATIONAL	4033954
LIVERPOOL (JOHN LENNON)	3986654
ABERDEEN	3723662
LONDON CITY	3647824
LEEDS BRADFORD	3274474
BELFAST CITY (GEORGE BEST)	2555145
SOUTHAMPTON	1831732
JERSEY	1495707
SOUTHEND	1102358
CARDIFF WALES	1023932
PRESTWICK	913685
GUERNSEY	894602
EXETER	767404
ISLE OF MAN	729703
DONCASTER SHEFFIELD	724885
BOURNEMOUTH	661584
INVERNESS	612725
NORWICH	458968

Source: CAA Website (May 2015) - * This is not the full definitive list of airports but a guide to passenger numbers at a selection of UK airports.

Table 4.3 - World Top Ten Passenger Carrying Airports 2013

Rank	City (Airport)	Total Passengers
1	ATLANTA GA, US (ATL)	92 389 023
2	BEIJING, CN (PEK)	78 675 058
3	LONDON, GB (LHR)	69 433 565*
4	CHICAGO IL, US (ORD)	66 701 241
5	TOKYO, JP (HND)	62 584 826
6	LOS ANGELES CA, US (LAX)	61 862 052
7	PARIS, FR (CDG)	60 970 551
8	DALLAS/FORT WORTH TX, US (DFW)	57 832 495
9	FRANKFURT, DE (FRA)	56 436 255
10	HONG KONG, HK (HKG)	53 328 613

*Source: Airport Council International (2015) *73405330 (CAA: 2015)*

Conclusions

The role of airports is essential within the commercial aviation sector. Problems of congestion at major hub airports have forced governments and airlines to look at how best to serve passengers by using regional airports instead. It is worth noting however that international airports such as London Heathrow need to have critical mass. Without this, the ability to operate certain routes would not be possible in the absence of both high demand from UK residents and the use of international transfer passengers.

References and Suggested Further Reading

Airport Council International (2015) www.aci.aero

CAA (2015) www.caa.co.uk

Graham, A. (2008) Managing Airports – An International Perspective, 3rd Ed, Butterworth-Heinemann.

KLM Airlines (2012) www.klm.com

Lober, T. (2004) General Aviation Small Aerodrome Research Study, The Bartlett School, University College London

Robin Hood Doncaster Airport (2008) www.robinhoodairport.com

Ryanair (2015) www.ryanair.com

Wells, A.T. & Young, S. (2003) Airport Planning and Management, 5th Edition, McGraw-Hill Professional.

Unit Five

Commercial Aircraft Manufacturers

Unit Objectives:

On completing this unit, you should be able to:

- Distinguish between the main commercial aircraft manufacturers
- Explain the current and future products offered by the main aircraft manufacturers
- Describe the selection criteria used by airlines when purchasing new aircraft

Introduction

The building of jet and turboprop aircraft is a highly complex and expensive business. The specialisations required to undertake this process have seen the market within the western world being reduced to just two companies for any aircraft order over 150 seats, namely Airbus Industries and Boeing. The same is also true for the 50 to 100 seat market with Bombardier and Embraer being the only major choices available today. This market is, however, changing with Japan, China and Russia all developing small commuter/regional aircraft for operation. The Russian Sukhoi Superjet 100 undertook its first commercial flight in April 2011 with Armavia. There are currently 240 orders for the Superjet which places it well behind the dominating companies within this market area of Bombardier and Embraer.

This unit will look at the current providers of aircraft to the commercial aviation industry and the portfolio of products offered for sale. It will initially look at the jet airliner market before turning its attention to the commuter / regional marketplace.

The unit will finish by looking at what factors airlines have to take into consideration when purchasing aircraft. The cost of aircraft is just one of a number of factors that airlines have to get right so as to make sure that these highly expensive and complex pieces of equipment will serve them well over a twenty to thirty year period.

Airbus Industries

Airbus Industrie was established in 1970 as a partnership between European aerospace companies from France, Britain and Germany as a way of competing more successfully against the American companies of Boeing, McDonnell Douglas (purchased by Boeing) and Lockheed (which has stopped commercial aircraft manufacturing). In 1971, the Spanish government entered the partnership through its aircraft manufacturing initiative CASA. In 2000, the German, French and Spanish partners merged to create EADS with an 80% stake in Airbus, the remaining 20% being controlled by BAE Systems of the UK. By 2006, BAE Systems believed the time was right to leave the partnership and sold its share of the business to EADS which has since gained 100% control of the consortium.

The first aircraft produced by Airbus was the Airbus A300 which undertook its inaugural flight in 1972 and entered commercial service in 1974. Orders for both the A300 and the A310 were initially less than impressive but in 1981 Airbus launched the technologically advanced A320 series of aircraft which catapulted the company to the top of the airline manufacturer's league. Boeing has long complained that Airbus has only been able to invest in the development of such advanced aircraft due to the grants and subsidies given to the company by the respective governments of France, Spain, Germany and the UK. These arguments have, on a number of occasions, drawn Europe and America into costly trade disputes.

The current production list from Airbus is illustrated in table 5.1. One of the main advantages for airlines in buying the Airbus family of aircraft is its cockpit commonality which means that pilots only need spend a limited amount of time getting used to the controls as they are the same in all models produced. This means that a pilot can upgrade from a single aisled A320 to the massive A380 aircraft in a very short period of time and at reduced expense for the airline. Furthermore, the Airbus family of aircraft have helped airlines reduce maintenance costs based on the commonality of components used.

Table 5.1 – Airbus Aircraft Currently in Production

Type	Number of Passengers	Number of Engines	Maiden Flight
A318	107	2	2002
A319	124	2	1995
A319 neo	124	2	2015 (expected)
A320	150	2	1987
A320 neo	150	2	2014
A321	185	2	1993
A321 neo	185	2	2015 (expected)
A330	253-295	2	1992
A340	239-380	4	1991
A350	270-350	2	2013
A380	550	4	2005

Source: Airbus (2015)

Despite the fact that the Airbus range of aircraft share excellent commonality, the same cannot be said to the production process which sees components being shipped from across Europe to assembly plants in Toulouse, France and Hamburg, Germany for final production. To serve the growing Asian market Airbus opened an assembly plant in China in 2008. A production line for the A320 family of aircraft will open in Mobile, Alabama in 2015.

Airbus has pinned its hopes for future aircraft development on the Airbus A380 'super jumbo'. Having launched the product in 2002 in an attempt to outdo Boeing in its only remaining monopoly (based on the Boeing 747), the A380 underwent a number of teething problems relating to its weight and wiring. Airbus believes that this aircraft will help airlines develop their network at busy international hub airports such as London Heathrow and New York JFK by increasing capacity through size rather than added frequencies. With current orders standing at 192, the A380 still has a long way to go to achieve the level of sales of the Boeing 747 that stand at over 1,500.

As highlighted in unit 2, during 2014 not one new order was taken for the A380 which many in the industry puts the future of the programme at great risk. The most likely candidate to take on more A380's is Emirates but its CEO Tim Clark has indicated that he is not prepared to do this unless Airbus reengineers the aircraft as the A380neo.

The company focus on the A380 has caused it to be late in its development proposals for a replacement aircraft for the A330/A340 family of jets. This has been resolved with the development of the A350 but has lost a substantial amount of ground to Boeing and its highly successful 787 project.

A US Airways A330 arrives at LHR (Photographed by the author)

Environmentally, Airbus has been at the forefront of developments to help reduce noise and air pollution. The use of composite materials and research into bio fuels are just some of the initiatives that Airbus has committed to. The company has also been a lead organisation within the European Union's Clean Sky Joint Technology Initiative (www.cleansky.eu)

Boeing

The Boeing Company can trace its routes back to its founding father William E. Boeing, who opened his first aerospace company in 1916. As one can image from a company with such a long and illustrious history, Boeing has been at the forefront of commercial aircraft manufacture since the development of the B247 in 1933. Other notable achievements include the first jetliner to reach a 1,000 orders in the form of the Boeing 727, and the Boeing 737 which has achieved over 6,000 orders making it by far the most successful aircraft ever built.

Probably the most famous of all Boeing aircraft is the 747 jumbo jet which first flew in January 1970. Updated versions include the 200/300/400 which have become the workhorse of airline intercontinental fleets. In 2005, Boeing launched the Boeing 747 -8 Intercontinental series as the next stage of the aircrafts lifecycle. The 747-8i has unfortunately not sold in the same way as its predecessors having only achieved passenger derivative orders from Lufthansa, Korean Air, Air China and Transaero.

During the 1980's, Boeing introduced the 757 and 767 and worked on developing the 777 model. With their focus on these medium to long range aircraft, rival manufacturer Airbus was able to steel business destined for a new version of the 727/737 through the technologically advanced design and performance of the A320 family. It took Boeing until the mid 1990's to introduce the 737NG (Next Generation) family of aircraft which brought in the types of technology that Airbus customers had become accustomed to. Boeing has actually used this, perhaps, negative point to their advantage as can be seen from figure 5.1. The 737NG did not take long to develop a leading presence within the low cost market with airlines including Southwest Airlines (who have 410- 737NG's in fleet or on order) and Ryanair (with 300 in fleet or on order).

Figure 5.1 – Boeing has used its late development of the 737NG family of jets to its advantage arguing that they have newer technologies than rival Airbus. It has undertaken the same strategy with the launch of the Boeing 737Max

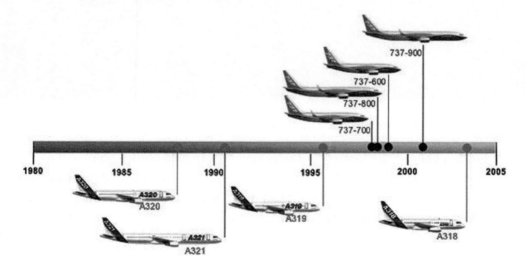

Source: www.boeing.com

The future of Boeing was to have been split between the 787 'Dreamliner' a long range aircraft which uses the very latest in material and avionic technologies to produce the smoothest and most environmentally efficient ride and the Boeing 747 -8. The 787 has been an enormous hit with airlines, achieving the fastest sales record for any airliner. This success has not, however, been matched by the Boeing 747-8. Currently, only one airline has ordered it for passenger services, Lufthansa who have placed an order for 20. Boeing's hopes of increasing this order were dashed in October 2007 when a loyal customer and the largest user of 747-400 aircraft, British Airways, signed an order with Airbus for the A380 aircraft.

Table 5.2 – Boeing Aircraft Currently in Production

Type	Number of Passengers	Number of Engines	Maiden Flight
737 600/700/800/900	132-215	2	1997
737 Max7/Max8/Max9	132-215 (est)	2	2017
747 – 400ER	416-524	4	1988 (400)
747 – 8I	467	4	2011
767	224-304	2	1981
777	400-451	2	1994
787	290-330	2	2011

Source: Boeing (2015)

Task 1

Investigate the cost of modern jetliners by visiting Boeing and Airbus websites. The table below will help you record the price of these aircraft.

Information available at the following web addresses (May 2015):

http://www.aircraftcompare.com

Model	Price ($)	Model	Price ($)
737 - 800		A321	
747 - 8		A330	
767 - 300ER		A340	
777 – 300ER		A350	
787 - 8		A380	

Do you believe the prices charged offer value for money? Compare and contrast the prices for similar models produced by the two manufacturers.

As we progress through 2015, the rivalry between Boeing and Airbus continues. Both are seeking to increase sales of aircraft in a period of uncertainty due to increasing fuel charges and consumer negativity based on environmental problems. Figure 5.2 looks at aircraft orders over the past eighteen years for both manufacturers which sees Airbus just ahead as it stands at the time of writing (May 2015).

Figure 5.2 – Airbus and Boeing Aircraft Orders 1990 – 2015

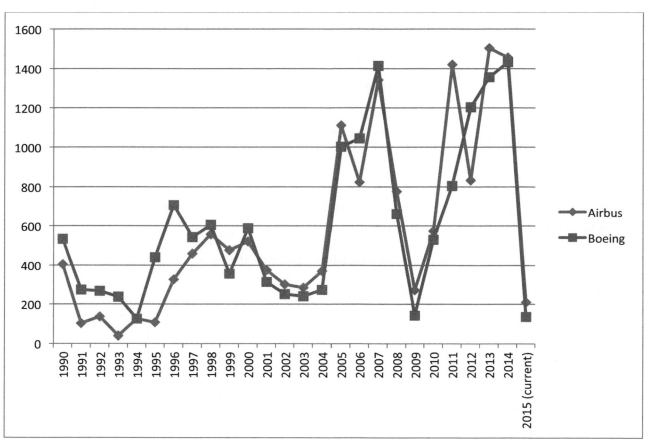

Source: Data collected from Boeing & Airbus Websites (May 2015)

The battle for the skies between Boeing and Airbus has caused a great deal of interest from within the industry. A number of texts have been created looking at this issue with Kenny Kemp (2007) profiling the market for the A380 versus the Boeing 787 in 'Flight of the Titans'.

Table 5.3 highlights aircraft type based on range and passenger capacity for both Airbus and Boeing aircraft.

Table 5.3 – Airbus v Boeing based on Passengers v Range

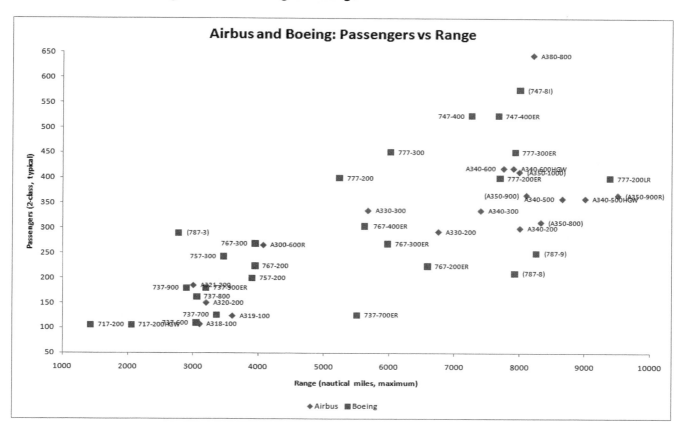

Source: Lcmortensen -
http://en.wikipedia.org/wiki/File:Airbus_and_Boeing_Passengers_vs_Range.png

An American Airlines Boeing 777 just after touch down at LHR (Photographed by the author)

The Next Short Haul Airliner - A320NEO or B737MAX

Both Airbus and Boeing have been slow to develop the 'next generation' of short haul jet aircraft to replace the aging design of the Airbus A320 and Boeing 737. The reasons behind this include the large order book that both manufacturers have for the current versions of their jets and both believe that there really needs to be a leap in technology to successfully develop the next generation of jet. This impasse has caused difficulties for airlines who want to plan their future fleets early so as to arrange the correct finance and strategically decide on what routes to serve.

The stalemate was broken in December 2010 when Airbus Industries announced the development of the Airbus A320neo – New Engine Option. This jet whilst not that much advanced in design from the current A320 will use the newly developed CFM International LEAP-X or Pratt & Whitney PW1000G engines. Other enhancements will include sharklets at the end of the wing tips. These and other advances in aircraft build will lead to a 15% efficiency improvement. At the time of writing (May 2015) almost 3,600 orders have been placed for the A320neo.

On discovering how well airlines took to the launch of the A320neo Boeing decided in August 2011 to launch the Boeing 737MAX. This variant utilises the same design as the current model but as with the A320neo uses new engines and wing design to create cost savings of 16% compared to current models. Almost 2,700 orders for this new variant of the Boeing 737 have been placed (May 2015).

Bombardier

Based in Montreal, Canada, Bombardier originally started out in 1937 building snowmobiles. It was not until 1986 that the company agreed the takeover of Canadair. Further purchases followed of deHavilland Canada, Shorts Brothers and Learjet probably the best known of the company's products which build business jets (Biz Jets).

Within commercial aviation, Bombardier has developed a number of successful commuter aircraft including the Dash 7 and Dash 8. Based on the success of these turbo prop aircraft, Bombardier has launched the next generation of 'Q' Series aircraft which are highly efficient, environmentally friendly and offer greater passenger comfort.

Bombardier has also introduced regional jet aircraft catering for the 70 – 100 seat aircraft market. The CRJ has been the most successful regional jet produced selling over 1,400 examples. The full production range of bombardier aircraft can be seen in table 5.4.

Table 5.4 – Bombardier Aircraft Currently in Production

Type	Number of Passengers	Number of Engines
CRJ 700	70	2
CRJ 900	88	2
CRJ 1000	100	2
Q200	37	2 Prop
Q300	50	2 Prop
Q400	70	2 Prop
CS100	125	2
CS130	145	2

Source: Bombardier Website (May 2015)

Bombardier has gained a reputation for being ultra environmentally friendly with the 'Q' Series of turboprop aircraft. So much so, that one UK Low Cost operator www.flybe.com has introduced an energy rating scheme similar to that operated by domestic appliance regulations. Figure 5.3 shows the Eco rating scheme introduced by www.flybe.com.

Figure 5.3 – Example of the Eco Rating scheme for the Bombardier Q400

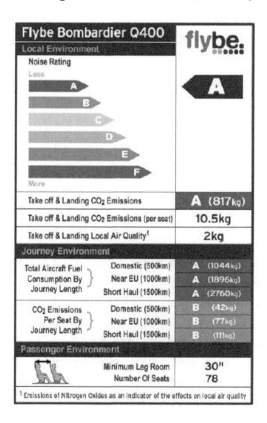

Source: www.flybe.com

Embraer

Empresa Brasileira de Aeronautica S.A, or Embraer, was established in Brazil in 1969. For the first decade of operation, the company concentrated on the production of military aircraft and a derivative of this, the EMB – 110 Bandeirante, for commercial use. The 1980's saw the successful launch of the EMB – 120 Brasilia turboprop commuter aircraft which won export orders from across the globe. Production of the Brasilia only stopped in 2002.

During 1990 the company produced plans for a new generation of turbofan aircraft capable of operating regional routes efficiently, with a high level of passenger comfort at faster speeds than the traditional turboprops used on such services. The creation of the ERJ 145 was a welcome boost to commuter airlines with over 900 examples of this variant being sold.

As a natural progression to the ERJ 135/145 series of aircraft in 1999, Embraer started work on the E – Jet concept capable of taking between 70 and 110 passengers. The first E170 made its maiden flight in 2002 and the series has performed well against competition from Bombardier and the CRJ family of aircraft. Table 5.4 lists the current production list of Embraer aircraft.

Table 5.4 – Embraer Aircraft Currently in Production

Type	Number of Passengers	Number of Engines
ERJ 135	37	2
ERJ 140	44	2
ERJ 145	50	2
ERJ 170	70	2
ERJ 175	88	2
ERJ 190	100	2
ERJ 195	122	2

Source: Embraer Website (May 2015)

The Aircraft Purchasing Process

The decision to purchase a jetliner is an expensive one as can be seen from task 1 within this unit. A number of decisions have to be made which will influence the decision of an airline as to which aircraft and variant is the best fit for their current and future route network. The main decision areas that will be investigated during this process are listed in Table 5.5 below. For a full review of how the decisions process is reached you are recommended to read Paul Clark's text 'Buying the Big Jets'. Another problem for airlines is that when you place an order for an airliner you can expect to receive it, not in terms of months, but often years. Both Boeing and Airbus have large order books currently for most of their aircraft types which further delays the delivery of aircraft. An airline ordering a brand new jet today can expect it to be in service probably not before 2016 at the very earliest.

Table 5.5 – Aircraft Purchasing Decision Key Variable

Criteria	Information
Cost	All costs are based in US $ which means that economies will find it cheaper to buy aircraft when their economy is stronger than the $.
Range	Airlines look to operate aircraft in certain flight envelopes depending on their route structure. A good range is critical in making this decision as it will allow greater future flexibility.
Passenger Capacity	Depending on the type of operation airlines will alter the characteristics of the cabin to suit their business model. For example, Ryanair operate the 737-800 in a 189 configuration compared to SAS which has 145 seats on average
Cabin Layout/Configuration	Airlines will configure their aircraft based on product concept. Airlines will try and allow flexibility on short haul services by operating a curtain system to separate classes.
Cargo Capacity	Cargo capacity will vary depending upon type of operation. Low cost and charter carriers tend not to carry cargo as it increases turnaround times.
Fleet Commonality	Due to increases in the cost of components and training for mixed fleet utilisation airlines have tended to look for fleet commonality to reduce operating expenditure.
Purchase or Lease	Due to the high fixed cost and lack of flexibility that purchasing aircraft entails, airlines have started using leasing agreements as a way of helping to reduce balance sheet liabilities.
Maintenance Costs and Considerations	Airlines are looking to purchase aircraft that have been granted extended periods of time between major overhauls.
Environmental Issues	The need to be 'green' is a major consideration for airlines looking to purchase aircraft. This has two affects, increases efficiencies and helps promotes a favourable image to the travelling public.
Airport Operating Envelope	Airlines need to make sure that the aircraft they purchase can land and manoeuvre safely at each airport they serve. The introduction of the Airbus A380 has had implication for taxiway width, gate height and strength of asphalt.

Task 2

Based on the cost and issues surrounding long delivery times for new aircraft, is there any other way airlines can introduce aircraft to their fleet?

For a clue visit the following website - http://www.gecas.com/en/

Conclusions

The manufacture of commercial airliners is highly complex one which involves risks of producing the right type of airliner at the right time. So great is the pressure on aircraft manufacturers today to produce ultra high technology, light weight and efficient aircraft, that Boeing have decided to wait at least another ten years before looking at revising their highly successful Boeing 737 family of jets.

References and Suggested Further Reading

Clark, P. (2007) Buying the Big Jets – Fleet Planning for Airlines, Ashgate Publishing.

Kemp, K. (2007) Flight of the titans, Virgin Books.

Visit Bombardier Inc at: http://www.bombardier.com/en/aerospace

Visit Embraer at: http://www.embraer.com/english/content/home/

Unit Six

Airline & Airport Technology

Unit Objectives:
On completing this unit, you should be able to:

- Identify the main technological developments within the commercial aviation industry
- Describe problems encountered whilst developing new technologies
- Explain why new technologies have been introduced for safety and economic considerations

Introduction

The commercial aviation industry is at the forefront of technology. Over the past decade, the industry has witnessed acceleration in the development of materials, avionics and power plants that have increased passenger and crew safety and led to more efficient operations. For example, the development of Traffic Alert and Collision Avoidance Systems (TCAS) has had a profound effect on both safety and operational efficiency. Aircraft fitted with these devices are warned when another aircraft strays into its flight envelope but at the same time they allow aircraft to fly closer together as computers monitor each other's flight's characteristics.

Other technologies have not been so successful, an example being Head-Up Displays. These have proved highly useful on fighter aircraft as they show the pilot all essential information without them needing to take their eyes off the terrain. The use of such technology within the commercial airlines has proved to be less than practical and has instead found its way as a novelty into premium car ranges.

The following table breaks down the industry into its component parts and highlights some of the latest technological developments that have aided flight operations or passenger handling.

Table 6.1 – Technological Developments within Commercial Aviation

Sector	Development
Airline	• Development of e-Ticketing – passengers are no longer given paper which can be lost but an electronic personal reference (PNR). Airlines have introduced mobile and PDA check-in through the use of a bar code sent to your phone at the time of booking or check-in. Airlines have also introduced Self Service Kiosks at airports allowing passengers greater say over their seating and reducing the need for check-in staff. • Computer Reservation Systems → Global Distribution System Versus Web bookings – more and more airlines are trying to channel bookings through their own website thereby cutting commission costs and allowing them to build profiles of their customers. Today's GDS's have undergone consolidation to allow them to contribute in a more competitive environment. • In-flight Entertainment (IFE) – jointly developed product between airlines and manufacturers. Current innovations include, portable DVD devices with gambling capabilities, the ability to access email and the internet and, perhaps even more controversially, the use of mobile phones on-board. • En-suite cabins – currently in use by a range of airlines including Emirates which will give premium class passengers a room with shower and toilet cubical as well as seat and bed. Will only be available on the A380 product. These ideas have, been thought of before with little real interest from the public. For example, Virgin Atlantic dreamt up the idea of a disco within the cargo area of their A340 – 600 aircraft, but the idea never left the planning stage. Suites are, however, becoming common with both Singapore Airlines and Jet Airways offering such products. Etihad Airlines has just introduced the concept of the 'residence by Etihad' the first time rooms have been offered on-board a commercial airliner with private bedroom and personal butler! • Required Navigation Performance (RNP) – satellite based navigation system which will allow aircraft to fly preciously between two points. The development of this system has taken time but may in the not too distant future reduce the need for air traffic control input and allow aircraft to judge speeds so as to reduce congestion at arrival airports. • Virgin Galactic – established in 2004 this Virgin brand will look at creating the first 'space tourists' as customers are placed into a sub orbital cruise. As of May 2015 test flights are suspended due to a fatal crash of its test craft.

Airport	<ul><li>Radio Frequency Identification (RFID) – a metallic strip is attached to baggage which, when it passes through sensors, identifies the passenger, flight number and the bags final destination. These chips have become common within retail, normally being attached to expensive household items such as perfumes, DVD's and razor blades within supermarkets.</li><li>Bluetooth Technology – by activating your mobile phone's Bluetooth facility certain airports are able to inform you of gate numbers and final calls. It also helps the airports by tracking you through the system and what you do.</li><li>Automatic Baggage Systems – Copenhagen Airport has introduced a baggage handling system that can take a bag from check-in to the hold of the aircraft with no human handling needed. It relies on the use of RFID technologies.</li><li>Security Scanning – from biometric data to equipment that can sniff for explosives. Airports are constantly developing technologies that make flying safer and speed up the security checking process.</li><li>Airport simulator – London Heathrow has developed a 360 degree simulator which allows Air Traffic Controllers to be trained in a virtual world.</li><li>Foreign Objects & Debris (FOD) Radar – the need for such equipment came to light after the Air France Concorde Crash caused by an object which had fallen from a Continental Airlines DC-10. Radar scans the runways to ensure no objects are left after each take off.</li><li>WiFi and WiMax operations – enable laptop computers and staff PDA systems to gain access to internet and intranet.</li><li>Geographic Information Systems (GIS) – allows mapping and data analysis of airport vehicles and aircraft.</li><li>Common Ramp Information Display Systems (RIDS) – Developed to coordinate the turnaround of aircraft with all staff having access to the same information as to destination, flight time, passenger numbers and time to departure.</li></ul>

Aircraft Manufacturing	<ul><li>Development of composite materials – make aircraft lighter i.e. fuel efficient and at the same time increase the strength of the fuselage</li><li>Power plant development – companies such as Rolls Royce, Pratt & Whitney and General Electric, CFM International and Snecma are all working on reducing carbon dioxide (CO_2) and nitrogen oxide (Nox), whilst making engines quieter, more powerful and efficient.</li><li>Bio fuel and hydrogen tests – The development of carbon free engines is currently concentrating on bio fuels. Virgin Atlantic has already undertaken one proving flight to show that the technology works. Environmentalist need to be convinced that the use of such technology is not just shifting the problem from the air to land use issues. The development of hydrogen fuel cells for airliners but been all but dropped due to its difficulty in being transported.</li><li>Passenger Comfort – The Boeing 787 incorporates anti turbulence devices and windows which automatically self tint so there is no need for blinds (also an advantage to airlines as they reduce weight).</li><li>Aircraft Communication Addressing and Reporting System (ACARS) – links the Flight Management System (FMS) on board the aircraft with the ground station. This enables operations to have live information as to the aircraft's status and maintenance information regarding the aircraft's serviceability.</li></ul>

Tasks

Based on the above table there are a number of questions that you should attempt below:

1. *What are the names and owners of the three biggest Global Distribution Systems in operation today? How have they looked to develop their products to compete with bookings through airline's own websites?*

2. Go to Singapore Airlines and Jet Airways websites and compare and contrast the products offered within their premium suites (www.singaporeair.com & www.jetairways.com).

3. How can airports use information gathered via Bluetooth and RFID technology to improve the layout and facilities offered at airports?

4. What are the main problems encountered with the use of bio fuels for commercial aircraft?. How can these issues be resolved?

5. *How has the use of ACARS helped airlines manage aircraft operations and maintenance?*

6. *What are the main underlying reasons for the late entry into service of both the Airbus A380 and Boeing 787?*

Conclusions

The technologies used with commercial aviation are advancing rapidly in the face of safety and environmental concerns. The use of new lightweight composite materials has proven to be a bonus from the point of view of operational efficiency and from a safety perspective. Airlines are constantly developing new product ideas to help attract new passengers, although, some of the ideas have yet to be proved. Airports have also needed to develop new technologies so as to combat the threat of terrorism. The introduction of passenger and baggage scanners which allow staff to examine suspect items with the use of technology will improve the detection rate.

As with any technology, one of the big issues for airlines, airports and even manufacturers is the cost and time of introducing these new developments. This has in some instances caused problems, as can be seen from the development of the Airbus A380 and Boeing 787 airliners.

References and Suggested Further Reading

CFM International website: http://www.cfm56.com/

IATA has developed a fact sheet look at the advantages of Self service kiosks:
http://www.iata.org/stbsupportportal/cuss/CUSSbackground.htm

Pratt & Whitney website: http://www.pw.utc.com/vgn-ext
templating/v/index.jsp?vgnextoid=047d34890cb06110VgnVCM1000004601000aRCRD

Rolls-Royce website: http://www.rolls-royce.com/civil_aerospace/default.jsp

Snecma website: http://www.snecma.com/index2.php?&lang=fr&lang=en

To find information on airport technologies go to: http://www.airport-technology.com/

 To see how an engine works go to the following web address on Pratt & Whitney's site:
http://www.pw.utc.com/vgn-ext-
templating/v/index.jsp?vgnextoid=ce7d0ac19a27a110VgnVCM100000c45a529fRCRD

What to become the first 'Space Tourist' visit: http://www.virgingalactic.com/

Unit Seven

Airport Operations

Unit Objectives:
On completing this unit, you should be able to:

- Identify the role of airport operations
- Explain the functions of an airport
- Describe the main service operators found at international airports
- Highlight the operational procedures undertaken by air traffic control

Introduction

This unit will look at the functionality and operational characteristics of an airport. It will first look at the role of airports before looking at the different service providers which are an integral part of the airport operation. Doganis (2003) illustrated that, contained within an airport, are a "wide range of services and facilities ....which can be divided into three distinct groups: essential operational services, traffic-handling services and commercial activities."

The unit will finish with an insight into the role of Air Traffic Control at airports and how they manage the flow of arriving and departing flights.

The role of an airport

The role of an airport is complex and for international gateway airports such as London Heathrow handling over 73,000,000 passengers a year, the problems can be immense. However, the reality is that airports serve two primary purposes. The first is to act as an interchange which allows passengers to transfer between transport modes. The second is to undertake the administrative roles essential for enabling a passenger to board their flight.

Interchange procedure

Most airports will seek good linkage to other transport infrastructure. This primarily will entail road access for the use by private cars, taxis and public bus and coach services. For hub airports the development of rail and underground lines are also seen as being important to help reduce congestion via road transportation and allow quicker links to the rest of the country (e.g. at Frankfurt Main Airport high speed ICE trains link passengers into the rest of the German rail network).

The need for airports to consider their environmental footprint has seen the increasing promotion of public transport services. A case in point is London Heathrow where bus lanes have been implemented and HAH, the airport's operator has, subsidised a local train service from central London which calls at all the main stops to Heathrow (the Heathrow Connect).

Administrative Procedure

The airport administrative procedure starts as the passenger enters the terminal. Today, it is common for certain passengers to have already undertaken the check-in process online thereby reducing the amount of processing required. For most passengers entry into the terminal can be represented systematically as highlighted in figure 7.1.

Figure 7.1 - The passenger administration process

Landside

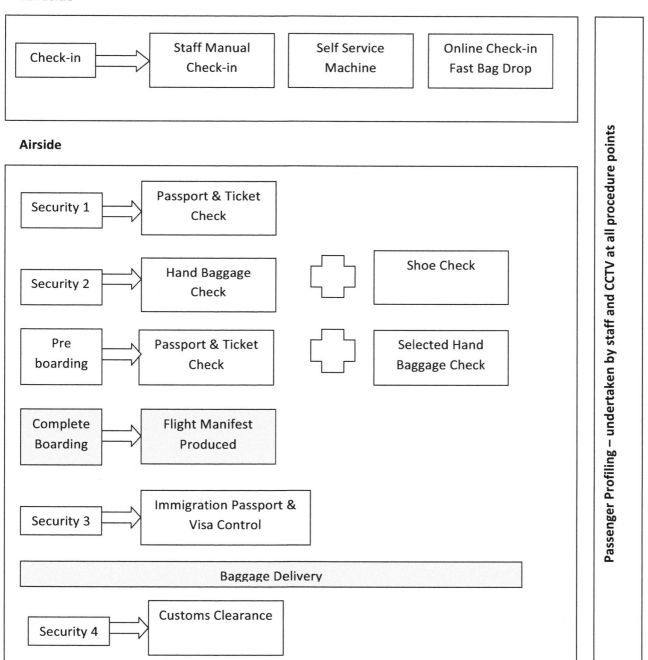

Airside

Airport Service Providers

Airport service providers are numerous and include those that are passenger oriented and those which deal specifically with the operation of the airport and aircraft. The ownership of these facilities is broken down into those owned and controlled directly by the airport or airline and those controlled by external companies.

Airport operators provide a variety of services including passenger information points, duty free shops and car parking. The final two have, however, often been sub contracted to external companies to run on their behalf (e.g. NCP runs the car parks at LHR). One of the main ways airports will generate revenue is through the retail offer provided. As retail is a highly specialised area, airports have invited major shopping chains to operate as concessionaires. This entails the retailer establishing a shop at the airport and paying the airport operator a percentage of the profit as well as rent for the property.

Airport operators will also provide security staff and emergency service provision such as fire and rescue units. Airports may also provide the provision of air traffic control and meteorology services.

Airlines tend to provide the services which are essential to securing the passenger experience and allowing them to operate efficiently. Therefore airlines will often run their own passenger oriented services such as, check-in facilities, lounges and catering services. Here again airlines have started to sub contract these services out to Ground Handling Agents to help reduce cost. Airlines, for example, only tend to run their own check-in at their hub airports and where the frequency of daily departures warrants employing their own staff. The main Ground Handling Companies found at London Heathrow are listed below:

- ASIG
- Aviance
- Cobalt Ground Solutions – part of the Air France/KLM Group
- DNATA
- Menzies Aviation
- Omni-Serv
- Swissport

Airlines, operationally, will employ their own maintenance facilities at hub airports but will rely on alliance partners or sub contract out this work at overseas facilities through Maintenance and Ground Support Agreement (MAGSA) to ground handling companies. At London Heathrow, British Airways maintains extensive engineering facilities (figure 7.2) which can overhaul every type of aircraft within the fleet. Airlines will also tend to employ the following ramp services:-

- Pushback Tugs
- Cargo and Luggage equipment
- Ground Power Units (where stand power or APU not available)
- Air Conditioning

- Water Supply
- De-icing (subcontracted in regions where snow and ice are not common to airport)

Figure 7.2 – Part of the extensive BA maintenance facilities at London Heathrow (photographed by the author)

The use of sub contractors within the airline and airport industry has grown dramatically over the past two decades as operators look to cut costs. The types of services that have been contracted out vary greatly based on how much product control an airline wants. The main services that have been successful sub-contracted are listed below:-

- Catering – large operators include LSG Sky Chefs and Gate Gourmet
- Fuel
- Sanitary Provision
- Crew buses – at London Heathrow for example TGM group

The operation of an airport will also require other service providers. These will include both public and private sector organisations. The main types of service are listed below:-

Public Sector Airport Service Provision

- Customs and Immigration
- Passenger and Cargo Data Collection
- Air Traffic Control (not all countries)
- Police, Ambulance and Fire Services
- Meteorological Services

Private Sector Airport Service Provision

- Telecommunications
- Gas and Electrical Supply

Task 1

Look back at the media reports covering the opening of London Heathrow Terminal Five. Make a list below of the main problems that caused the opening to go so wrong.

Air Traffic Control

Air Traffic Control (ATC) is one of the most technological advanced and complex areas of aviation. The role of ATC is to act as an advisory service to aircraft both on the ground waiting to taxi and take off and those in the air en-route to their destination and undertaking landing procedures.

The role of ATC can be broken down into two distinct criteria. Firstly, it is the role of ATC to make sure that aircraft keep a certain distance of separation between them. For air traffic controllers to do this they need not only think of the distance in front or behind (horizontal separation) but also the vertical separation between aircraft. Air traffic controllers are therefore highly skilled individuals who have an excellent mathematical ability to be able to think of a blip on a radar screen as a 3-D box travelling at speeds of over 300 mph. The second operational role ATC provide is to ensure a continuous flow of aircraft based on the conditions at an airport or en-route. The flow rate at London Heathrow for example operates at an incredible take off or landing every 90 seconds.

Apart from separation and flow rate ATC will also provide pilots with additional information required for safe flight operations including radar positioning information, weather conditions en-route and at destination airports, as well as providing navigation instructions and information.

Ownership of ATC varies depending on where you are in the world. In the UK, a public/private sector partnership NATS handles all flights en-route across UK airspace and airport ground movements at 15 airports including all London Airports. It is common for military controllers to direct commercial airliners in certain parts of the world especially where there are limited ground facilities.

Air Traffic Control divides its role into two operational areas, namely, terminal and airport control and en-route control. Terminal control deals with the landing and take-off clearance of aircraft as well as allowing engine start up, push back and taxi at the airport facility. Figure 7.3 shows the new London Heathrow Control Tower which allows controllers a full view of aircraft across this busy international airport. The role of en-route controllers is to guide aircraft from the climb phase of flight to the descent into the destination airport. Unlike terminal controllers these individuals tend to sit in highly computerised rooms such as the NATS Swanwick Centre in Hampshire which controls all air traffic across England and Wales as well as housing the London Area Control Centre (LACC) and the London Terminal Control Centre (LTCC).

The development of new technologies such as Global Positioning Satellites and computers on board aircraft have helped to reduce the separation limits required. These advances have been instrumental in allowing more aircraft to fly in the heavily congested air space above Europe and on the east coast of the US.

The European Union is working on developing further the use of The European Organisation for the Safety of Air Navigation (EUROCONTROL). It is this organisation's responsibility to deliver a seamless flow of aircraft across the European Union. The sovereignty of air space has meant, however, that it has not to date accomplished all of its objectives.

Task 2

Outline the main skills that are expected of an air traffic controller.

Figure 7.3 - The new imposing Air Traffic Control Tower at London Heathrow which gives controllers a full view of the airport including the newly developed Terminal Five (photographed by the author)

Conclusion

The operation of an airport is a highly complex procedure, but if done correctly, the passenger should notice no hold ups and feel themselves flowing through the facility effortlessly. It is only through the coordination of public and private sector companies that this is possible. This unit has highlighted the organisations required for the safe and efficient operation of an airport. Through task one you have been able to identify why, when these services do not work together, airports can become anything but an efficient interchange facility.

References and Suggested Further Reading

Ashford, N. *et al* (1997) Airport Operations, Second Edition, McGraw-Hill Professional.

Unit Eight

The Airline Product

Unit Objectives:
On completing this unit, you should be able to:

- Explain the purchase decision for both business and leisure flights.
- Discuss the differences between business and leisure passenger products
- Examine the different airline products available within the market
- Recognise the main customer experiences felt whilst travelling by air

Introduction

The conceptual thinking behind this unit is to ask why airline passengers buy certain airline products and what their expectation of them is. While this unit does involve a certain amount of basic marketing theory, it is in no way meant to reflect the comprehensive marketing literature available. For great depth within aviation marketing it is suggested that you read Shaw (2011) Airline Marketing and Management.

For us to understand the decisions made by the consumer as to what airline products to buy, we really need to start at the initial thought stage as to why passengers decide to fly and build upon this. To help us understand the process Figure 8.1 develops the process of the airline product planning route.

Figure 8.1 – Airline Product Purchasing Decision

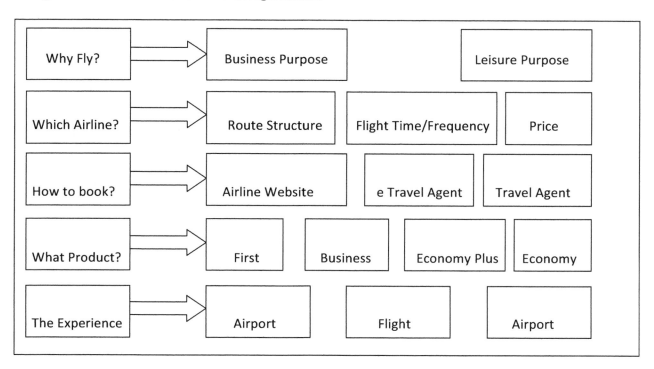

1. Why Fly?

The decision to fly or not will be affected by a number of different issues depending upon whether the passenger is looking to travel for business or leisure purposes. It is also important to remember that flying is not always the only means of transport available. Often, for domestic or intra-European journeys, it is sometimes quicker and more affordable to use other methods of transport such as the train, private car or coach.

Task 1

Air travel is often not the quickest or cheapest methods of transport. You are asked for this task to compare a journey from London to Manchester by air, train and coach. You will need to choose a day which is roughly 1 month away from today's date and to choose the cheapest fare available on that date. Look at the following table and complete the information requested

Method of transport	Price	Time Taken
Air LHR to MAN www.ba.com		
Train London Euston to Manchester Piccadilly www.virgintrains.co.uk		
Coach London Victoria Coach Station to Manchester www.nationalexpress.com or www.megabus.com		

Having undertaken this task, try it again, but this time look at the route London to Paris. Based on the sample principles as above, fill out the following table:

Method of transport	Price	Time Taken
Air LHR to CDG www.ba.com		
Train London St Pancras to Paris Nord www.eurostar.com		

For business travellers, the decision to fly is often not up to them but is required in order to attend a meeting with a potential client or network at an important conference. The business traveller does not pay for their ticket as it is undertaken as part of their work. The price that they are therefore willing to pay does not often reflect their personal circumstances. Business passengers tend to fly at 'peak' periods so as to allow them to spend as much time at home rather than lengthy periods away in hotels. For important meetings it is a good idea that they arrive feeling relaxed and refreshed. Airlines have developed specific cabins on-board the aircraft which look at allowing such travellers to unwind if they wish or undertake essential work with plug-ins for their laptop and even internet communication.

On the ground, business travellers have priority check-in desks. Companies such as Virgin Atlantic pick up passengers from their home or office and transport them to the airport. During the journey they are checked in and on arrival are whisked straight through security to the airport lounge (this service can be viewed at the following web address:

http://www.youtube.com/watch?v=tjLjHKLOcEc).

The use of business lounges at airports has become an important bonus for business executives as it is their last chance to catch up on email or print out documents before the flight. British Airways at their new Terminal Five lounges, also offer business class passengers the use of showers and spas just in case they would prefer to relax before the flight rather than work.

To keep such important customers loyal, major airlines have introduced 'Frequent Flyer Programmes' (FFP). The concept of these schemes is to offer preferential services to card holders in return for them remaining loyal to that company. Advantages offered include the use of airline lounges, upgrades, discounts on car hire and hotel facilities.

Task 2

Visit www.ba.com and www.emirates.com and look at their respective Frequent Flyer Programmes. Fill out the advantages offered to members based on the following tiers:

Membership Tier	BA Executive Club Rewards Offered	Emirates Skywards Rewards Offered
Blue		
Bronze		
Silver		
Gold		

If you were a business traveller based on the awards offered which would be your preferred airline and why?

The time of travel and the class of travel tend to be very different to leisure travellers. Travel by air for leisure purposes depends on the motivation for the trip and, as Holloway (2007) states, "when airlines are bidding for business from the holiday or vacation traveller, they are competing for the person's disposable time and disposable income." The motivational reasons to travel by air can be broken down into the following categories:

- For rest and relaxation – holiday
- Visiting Friends and Relatives (VFR)
- To attend sporting events – Olympic Games or Football World Cup
- Visit historical destinations – e.g. Coliseum in Rome or Pyramids in Egypt
- Travel for health reasons – undertake surgical procedures
- Shopping weekends – Paris or even New York

Whereas business passengers tend to be a small group of regular travellers, leisure travellers tend to travel infrequently with some having never travelled before. It is fair to say that for some leisure travellers the flight is as much a highlight of the holiday as the destination itself. Leisure travellers are still, however, an important market for airlines. British Airways (2008) points to the fact that leisure passenger volume accounts for 62% of all passengers as illustrated in Figure 8.2

Figure 8.2 – British Airways Passenger Volumes 2007

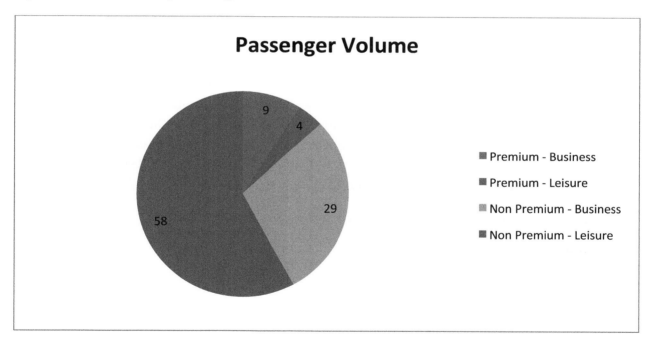

Sources: British Airways – Investor Day 2008

To cater specifically for the needs of leisure travellers, charter airlines were developed. However, today it is also very common to find tour operators booking seats on board scheduled flights as new and exotic destinations have become popular. Leisure travellers have also become more discerning and expect a higher level of product which has lead to charter airlines introducing upgraded cabins such as Thomson Airways Premium - www.thomsonflysenses.co.uk/. The traditional scheduled carriers have also realised that certain leisure passengers are prepared to pay a little more to enjoy extra leg space and a higher quality of in-flight service. Examples here include Virgin Atlantic with

Premium Economy (http://www.virgin-atlantic.com/en/gb/whatsonboard/premiumeconomy/index.jsp) and British Airways with World Traveller Plus (http://www.britishairways.com/travel/world-traveller-plus/public/en_gb).

Case Study – Air Miles to Avios

Whilst leisure travellers will not find it beneficial to join a frequent flyer programme there are still ways that free flights can be obtained without having to travel on a frequent basis. The development of Air Miles during 1988 has helped over 8 million consumers gain points which can be used for purchasing flights. Originally set up by British Airways and a partner organisation, the airline has since taken full control of the operation. As such it should come as no surprise that the best deals tend to be on less busy BA flights. It therefore acts as a good way of reducing capacity on less popular flights. The scheme initially operated as a loyalty programme with a handful of selected retail partners. Today, Air Miles operates in much the same way but also allows consumers to earn points by 'clicking through' its website to a vast range of e-retailers to accrue points on their purchases.

In September 2011 the decision was taken to rebrand Air Miles to reflect the more 'international' needs of British Airways, due mainly, to its integration into the International Airline Group with Iberia of Spain. The rebranding has furthermore, seen British Airways merging its highly successful Executive Club into the Avios portfolio. Customers can now save air miles either by flying or shopping with all points being stored at a central account. Customers have nevertheless been sceptical about the merged operation as they now have to pay all taxes for flights undertaken, this was not the case under the old Air Miles scheme.

More information is available at: http://www.avios.com/

2.   Which Airline?

The decision as to which airline to fly with will be affected by the route network offered. Airlines such as Lufthansa have vast global networks covering some 220 destinations in 81 countries. The development of airline alliances has allowed Lufthansa to increase the number of destinations it serves to 1,356 destinations in 193 countries (Lufthansa Website, May 2015).

The use of airline alliances has also allowed companies such as Lufthansa to offer a high level of frequency on routes which is of paramount importance to business travellers and also helps tempt leisure travellers based on the timings offered.

The importance of route network is of greatest importance to business travellers. For the leisure market, it is also imperative to think about the price of the trip. Being highly elastic, the leisure traveller will not book if the price of the ticket is deemed to be to high and will look for alternative or substitute products instead.

3. How to Book?

The booking of airline seats has undergone a revolution over the past decade with consumers having easier access to the Internet. Originally developed by the low cost airlines such as easyJet and to help reduce administration costs (including travel agent commission, ticketing costs and general sales force), the Internet has seismically changed the booking habits of air travellers. Although the low cost carriers once dominated the Internet, traditional airlines such as British Airways have been quick to catch up. With successful marketing campaigns including 'have you clicked yet', BA estimates that over 40% of passengers book online. This is still, however, far short of Ryanair who can boast that 99% of its passengers book online.

Task 3

Why do airlines want to move passengers away from booking with travel agents and e-travel agents and to book directly with them?

4.   What Product?

Airlines offer different products depending on the type of operation undertaken. Table 8.1 highlights the types of product offered by the main passenger carrying airlines.

Table 8.1 – Product Classes offered by Commercial Airlines

Traditional Scheduled Airline	Low Cost	Charter Airline
First	-	-
Business	*	**
Economy Plus	*	Economy Plus (long haul)
Economy	Economy	Economy

*Certain Low Cost Carriers have introduced services that are specifically aimed at business travellers – easyJet is a good example here.

**Charter carriers have introduced on their long haul services separate cabins that offer services akin to a traditional airlines economy plus/ business class cabin.

The above table is a very simplified version as many variations can be found within the sector. For example, Air Canada scrapped its first class product over a decade ago and instead offers an Executive First product which charges business class fares but looks to emulate the first class offer. At the opposite end of the spectrum, Singapore Airlines has revamped its first class product on-board the Airbus A380 by offering private suites.

Task 4

Taking British Airways as the example what do you think passengers are looking for from the following product range? To help you answer this task visit www.ba.com

Product Type	Service Expectation
First	
Club World	
World Traveller Plus	
World Traveller	
Euro Traveller	

Task 5

Ancillary revenue has become an important aspect of the commercial aviation sector over the past decade. Define what Ancillary Revenue means and highlight what types of products airlines sell via such methods?

5. The Experience

The passenger experience is the whole process of choosing the right airline, based on route, price, booking system, classes of travel available and finally the journey itself. The first few categories can be judged easily in some instances as an airline either flies point to point or not, and the fare offered can be judged against what other companies are offering. The problem with class of product offered and the journey itself is that they are individual and therefore highly subjective. Factors such as the time of day, month or season can have a highly influential impact on the overall travel experience. For example, at Christmas travelling is always going to involve longer queues due to the sheer volume of travellers. This will obviously count against the experience of travelling at that time of year. When on-board, passengers will also have a very different impression of the cabin based on an individual's anatomy. Influences such as height, mean that anyone over six foot will always find it difficult to get comfortable in economy class based on a 32" seat pitch.

To help passengers choose the best possible seat for themselves on the right airline, there are a number of both independent and airline operated websites which can help. At the outset of the booking process an organisation by the name of Skytrax allows travellers to read airline reviews as well as seeing their ranking. The company also judges airport facilities such as lounges, shops and the ease of travelling through such facilities. Further information can be found at www.airlineequality.com. To find the best seat on an aircraft the website trip advisor has developed the 'seat guru' (www.seat guru.com). From the seat guru website, you can look at all the major international carriers and decide on the best seat for your journey as illustrated in figure 8.3.

Figure 8.3 – Seat Guru map for Virgin Atlantic Airbus A340-600

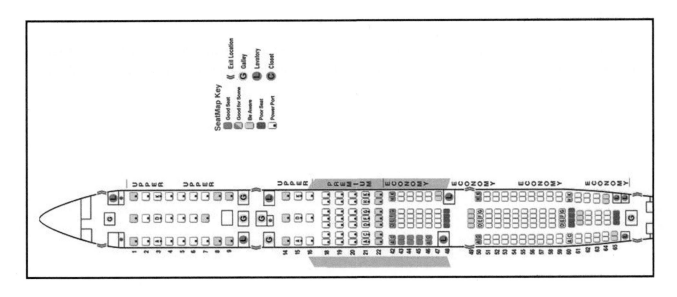

(Source: Seat Guru at
www.seatguru.com/airlines/Virgin_Atlantic_Airways/Virgin_Atlantic_Airways_Airbus_A340_2.php)

Airlines look to aid the passenger experience by reducing the stresses and strains of the airport process. They look to achieve this via the following methods:

- Introduction of online check-in or the use of check-in kiosks at the airport
- Ability to choose your seat either at the time of booking or at check in with the use of seat maps as illustrated in figure 8.4

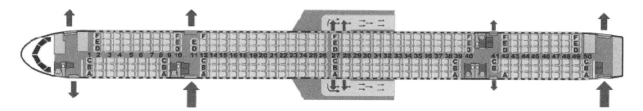

Figure 8.4 - Typical seat map for a Boeing 757 aircraft (Source: Condor Airlines)

- Heathrow's Terminal five operates on a flow system so passengers do not have to double back on themselves and can see the finishing line i.e. the gate almost as soon as they have entered the terminal (the reality is, however, somewhat different).

For passengers who do not travel frequently the idea of going to an airport and being subjected to a number of strange processes can be an ordeal if not a highly upsetting time, especially if the passenger is also fearful of flying. Airports and airlines therefore try to make the experience as hassle free as possible. The interaction between airport, airline staff and the passenger is vital within this role with customer service training being one of the main priorities for all commercial aviation organisations.

Task 6

Think of the airport process as a continuum; on the graph below highlight what you think are the most stressful times for infrequent passengers travelling through a busy international gateway airport.

Stress
Factor

Car Parking – Enter Terminal – Check-in – Security – Waiting for flight – Called to Gate – Boarding

Conclusions

The airline product is complex and involves both external as well as internal processes to produce the final experience (used here as the term product simplifies the production of this good). In order for passengers to have an excellent experience, it takes great coordination between the different organisations. When it works, passengers should feel that the flow through the system is painless (see unit seven). Where it does not work the whole process is disrupted and depending on the severity of the problem could mean the loss of that passenger for good!

References and Suggested Further Reading

Coutts Clay, J. (2006) Jetliner Cabins, 2nd Edition, John Wiley and Sons.

Lovegrove, K. (2000) Airline: Identity, Design and Culture, Laurence King Publishing.

Shaw, S. (2011) Airline Marketing and Management, 7th Ed, Ashgate Publishing.

Visit British Airways Investor Day 2008 Presentation at http://library.corporate-ir.net/library/69/694/69499/items/282903/Investor_Day_6March08_Pres.pdf

Unit Nine

Commercial Aviation Law

Unit Objectives:

On completing this unit, you should be able to:

- Explain the main aviation laws to affect passenger rights
- Understand the terms of the EU's Denied Boarding legislation
- Discuss the historical significance of the Chicago Convention
- Explain the Freedoms of the Air
- Recognise the criteria required to gain a UK CAA Air Operators Certificate and Licence
- Evaluate the importance to tourists of the Schengen Agreement

Introduction

The term aviation law covers a huge mix of both specific legislation affecting the industry as well as domestic and European legislation. Specific legislation that is pertinent to the study of commercial aviation will include the Chicago Convention and the UK Civil Aviation Authorities CAP regulations. Airlines and airports also need to address legislation that is specific to their home country and often to the countries to which they operate. Here we need to think about Consumer Law, Criminal Law, Administrative Law, Competition Law, Insurance Law and Health and Safety Law to name just a few.

The scope of this chapter will concentrate on the main legislation which directly affects commercial aviation based on consumer rights and UK airline and airport operations.

Task 1

Based on what we covered in Unit Two, Historical Perspectives, can you complete the dates missing from table 9.1?

Table 9.1 – Commercial Aviation Legislation Development

Date	Event
1919	Paris Air Navigation Convention
	Warsaw Convention
1944	Chicago Convention – Establishment of ICAO
	Bermuda Bilateral Agreement – US & UK
1955	The Hague Protocol
1971	Guatemala City Protocol – further amendments to Hague Protocol
	Bermuda II Bilateral Agreement – US & UK
1978	US Deregulation
	European Union - First Package for Air Deregulation
	European Union – Second Package for Air Deregulation
	European Union – Third Package for Air Deregulation
1999	Montreal Convention
	EU denied-boarding Compensation Scheme
	US – EU Open Skies Agreement

Aviation Consumer Law

1. The Warsaw Convention

One of the first pieces of law to affect aviation, the Warsaw Convention of 1929, as subsequently amended, sets out the liability for carriers carrying international passengers, their luggage or cargo.

For passengers, the Warsaw Convention is of particular importance based on its implication for loss luggage. The legislation put forward compensation amounts based on Special Drawing Rights (SDR's) that passengers could claim in the event of lost or mislaid baggage.

Whilst the Warsaw Convention was the first major legislation that affected air passengers it has since been replaced by the Montreal Convention on all ticketing and baggage receipts.

2. The Montreal Convention

The Montreal Convention of 1999 looked at updating the rules and regulations that affect the transport of passengers, baggage and cargo laid down by the Warsaw Convention of 1929. The Treaty revised numerous areas but is probably noteworthy based on the compensation scheme which was introduced for air disaster victims and their families. The European Union took responsibility for all member states in ratifying the Montreal Convention which came into force on 28th June 2004 under EU Regulation (EC) No. 2027/97 (as amended by (EC) No. 889/2002).

Task 2

Visit either British Airways website at www.ba.com or Virgin Atlantic Airways website at www.virgin-atlantic.com and highlight what passengers compensation rights are for the following categories:

Compensation in the case of death or injury	
Passenger delays	
Baggage delays	
Destruction, loss or damage to baggage	

3. European Union Denied-boarding Compensation Scheme

In 2004, the European Union introduced a clear scheme to help passengers through the myriad of legislation that affected their journey. All too often, airlines have used legislation laid down in the Warsaw Convention or Chicago Convention as a means of denying passengers recompense. Under the scheme, passengers are entitled to the following depending on if they have been denied boarding, had a flight cancelled or have experienced a long delay:-

Denied Boarding

It is the responsibility of the airline to initially look for volunteers to disembark from the flight due to overbooking. Any passenger who is willing to give up their seat must be compensated. Only after seeking volunteers and finding no willing candidates should airlines look at denying boarding. Any passenger who volunteers or is denied boarding are entitled to the following recompense:-

- € 250 for flights of less than 1500 km

- € 400 for intra-Community flights of more than 1500 km and for other flights 1500 and 3500 km

- € 600 for all other flights.

Apart from financial consideration, airlines have to offer passengers who volunteer or are denied boarding the following:

- the choice between reimbursement of their ticket and an alternative flight

- meals, refreshments and hotel accommodation.

Flight Cancellation

If an airline cancels a flight, passengers will be entitled to the same compensation as those who experience denied boarding. This is unless the carrier can prove one of the following, as laid down in EU regulations:

- they are informed two weeks before the scheduled time of departure, or

- they are informed in due time and re-routed at a time very close to that of their original flight.

In addition, in case of cancellations, passengers will receive three **other rights**:

- meals and refreshments;

- hotel accommodation, when a cancellation obliges a passenger to stay overnight; and

- reimbursement, when a cancellation delays a passenger for at least five hours.

Delayed Flights

When a flight is delayed for some period (see table 9.2) of time the airlines must, under EU regulations, offer:

- meals and refreshments;

- hotel accommodation, when a delay obliges a passenger to stay overnight; and

- reimbursement, when a delay delays a passenger for at least five hours.

Table 9.2 – EU Delayed Flights Criteria

Flight length	Delay
Flight less than 1,500 km	Over 2 hours
Flights of between 1,500 km to 3,500km plus all intra EU flights in access of 1,500 km	Over 3 hours
All non EU flights over 3,500 km	Over 4 hours

Task 3

What problems has the EU's Denied-boarding Compensation Scheme caused for both passengers and airlines? From an airlines point of view is this legislation fair based on today's operational targets?

Aviation Operation and Management Law

The Convention on International Civil Aviation – The Chicago Convention

Under the Chicago Convention signed in 1944, two important areas of aviation were dealt with. Firstly, the establishment of a world aviation body in the form of the International Civil Aviation Organisation (ICAO) which came into effect after ratification by member countries on the 5 March 1947. Secondly, it laid down a framework for the operation of international air services. The main idea was to create multi lateral treaties which would free up the sovereignty of the skies to, whoever wished to serve a specific destination. Whilst this may seem a fantastic idea today in 1944 the Second World War had only just ended in Europe and was still ongoing in the Pacific. Countries were therefore reluctant to lose the sovereignty of the skies above them. Therefore, instead of reaching multi-lateral deals the convention relied heavily on more complicated bi-lateral deals. To this day, the Bermuda Agreement between the United Kingdom and the United States remains a benchmark of what to include within such negotiations. For airlines to operate safely and efficiently from one country to another and to help direct bi-lateral negotiations the Chicago Convention developed nine freedoms of the air. These are highlighted in figure 9.1.

Apart from the freedoms of the air the other main areas covered by the Chicago Convention are highlighted below (Source: www.dft.gov.uk):

Article 1 - sovereignty of air space
Article 5 - covering charter flights
Article 6 - covering scheduled flights
Article 7 - restriction on cabotage
Article 15 - non-discriminatory *user charges*
Article 24 and Annex 9 - customs
Article 29 - documents to be carried on aircraft
Article 31 - certificates of airworthiness
Article 33 - recognition of certificates

The Chicago Convention is an ever changing piece of legislation which can be found at the following web address:

http://www.icao.int/icaonet/dcs/7300_cons.pdf

Figure 9.1 – The Freedoms of the Air

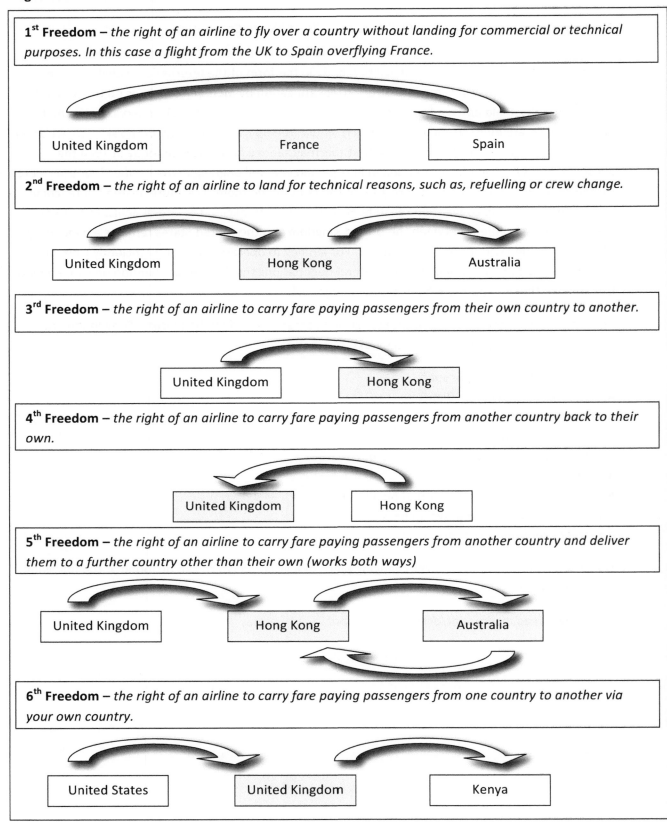

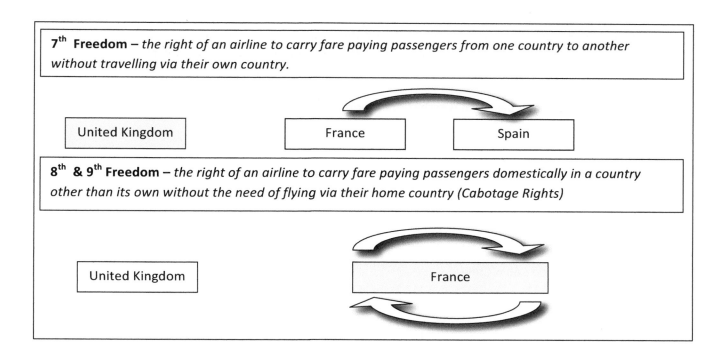

7th Freedom – *the right of an airline to carry fare paying passengers from one country to another without travelling via their own country.*

8th & 9th Freedom – *the right of an airline to carry fare paying passengers domestically in a country other than its own without the need of flying via their home country (Cabotage Rights)*

Within the Chicago Convention, the areas which are updated the most form its annex. The full list of this annex is highlighted below (Source: www.dft.gov.uk):

Annex 1 - Personnel licensing
Annex 2 - Rules of the Air
Annex 3 - Meteorological Services for International Air Navigation
Annex 4 - Aeronautical Charts
Annex 5 - Units of Measurement for Air and Ground Operations
Annex 6 - Operation of Aircraft
Annex 7 - Aircraft Nationality and Registration Marks
Annex 8 - Airworthiness of Aircraft
Annex 9 - Facilitation (expediting entry and departure at airports)
Annex 10 - Aeronautical Telecommunications
Annex 11 - Air Traffic Services
Annex 12 - *Search and Rescue*
Annex 13 - Aircraft Accident Investigation
Annex 14 - Aerodromes
Annex 15 - Aeronautical Information Services
Annex 16 - Environmental Protection
Annex 17 - Security - Acts of Unlawful Interference
Annex 18 - The Safe Transport of Dangerous Goods by Air.

Civil Aviation Authority – Air Operators Certificate

To operate a commercial aircraft within the UK the airline must hold a valid Air Operators Certificate which shows that they are competent to run such a venture. The main areas covered by the AOC include:

1. Qualification based on weather operations

2. Mass and Balance

3. Instrument and Equipment

4. Communication and Navigation

5. Aircraft Maintenance

6. Flight and Cabin Crew

7. Manuals , Logs and Records

8. Transport of dangerous goods

9. Security

Full information on obtaining a AOC can be found at the CAA website:

http://www.caa.co.uk/docs/1404/EU-OPS20080331.pdf

Civil Aviation Authority – Air Operators Licence

The CAA breaks Airline operation licensing down into two forms:

- Type A Licence – covers aircraft with 20 seats or above

- Type B Licence – covers aircraft with 19 or less seats

To hold a licence to operate an airline in the UK an airline must, in short, meet the following criteria:

1. The business must be based within the United Kingdom

2. The holder of the licence must be a resident of the European Economic Area (EEA). This includes all the European Union plus Iceland, Liechtenstein, Norway and Switzerland.

3. The holder must be able to prove that the company has the finance to operate through the first two years.

4. The holder must demonstrate that they have the correct insurance cover in place to cover any eventuality.

5. The holder must also be in possession of an Air Operators Certificate (AOC).

Other Important Legislation

The Schengen Agreement

An agreement established in 1985 in the town of Schengen with the aim of creating a common immigration policy and reduction of border controls within the Schengen Visa Area. The agreement allows tourists to apply for only one visa to travel to all Schengen countries. The UK and Ireland do not participate within this agreement. A total of 26 countries have signed up to the scheme but currently only the following countries participate in full:

Austria, Belgium, Denmark, Finland, France, Germany, Iceland, Italy, Greece, Luxembourg, Netherlands, Norway, Portugal, Spain and Sweden

Conclusions

The myriad of legislation that covers the airline industry has been developed since the first scheduled air services took place back in 1919. It has been amended, however, over the years to take into account passenger and cargo developments, as can be seen from table 9.1. These revisions have nevertheless taken place at a rather slow pace which has prompted organisations such as the European Union to introduce its own legislation to fill the gaps left by airlines. If airlines fail to deliver on other areas of consumer protection, further intervention by these organisations will occur.

References and Suggested Further Reading

Holloway, J.C. (2006) The Business of Tourism, Prentice Hall.

http://ec.europa.eu/transport/air_portal/passenger_rights/index_en.htm - for full information on EU passenger rights including denied boarding legislation.

Speciale, R.C. (2006) Fundamentals of Aviation Law, McGraw-Hill Professional.

Weber, L. (2007) International Civil Aviation Organization, Kluwer Law International.

www.caa.co.uk - for a full list of the regulations that affect UK airlines under the CAA CAP system.

www.eurovisa.info – information on Schengen Countries and visitor requirements.

Unit Ten

Commercial Aviation Regulatory Bodies

Unit Objectives:
On completing this unit, you should be able to:

- Identify the different global regulatory influences on commercial aviation
- Understand the intra European and domestic regulatory regime
- Recognise the reasons why commercial aviation is regulated

Introduction

International Civil Aviation has become used to a deregulated market in many parts of the world. The deregulation and liberalisation of air routes has not, however, stopped the need for regulation mainly based on the strict safety standards that passengers and crew expect. This unit will scrutinize the organisations that have been set up by both the public sector and private sector as a way of protecting and furthering the industry. Table 10.1 illustrates the main international organisation involved within the commercial aviation sector

Table 10.1 - International Civil Aviation Organisations

Organisation	Date Established	Ownership	Role
Airport Council International (ACI)	1970 (but current name and organisational structure ratified in 1991)	Trade Body (NGO)	<ul><li>Communicate good practice within the airport sector including the areas of:</li><li>Security</li><li>Safety</li><li>Environment</li><li>Advise on legislation</li></ul>
Association of European Airlines (AEA)	1952	European Trade Body (NGO)	<ul><li>Representative body for the main European scheduled airlines at the European Union and other IGO/NGO's organisations</li></ul>
European Aviation Safety Agency (EASA)	2003 Replaced the JAA (Joint Aviation Authority)	European Union (IGO)	<ul><li>Helps EU create aviation legislation</li><li>Grants type certification to new aircraft based on rigorous tests</li><li>Created a list of unsafe carriers who are not allowed to enter EU airspace</li></ul>

European Low Fares Airline Association (ELFAA)	2002	Trade Body	• To promote the interests of low cost airlines within Europe • Helps advise and direct policy makers within EU • Advises members on issues affecting Low Cost Airlines.
European Regional Airlines Association (ERAA)	1980	European Trade Body (NGO)	• Represents the values and aspirations of regional airlines within Europe.
Federal Aviation Administration (FAA)	1958	United States of America – Department of Transportation Federal Agency	• The most influential agency globally for aircraft and airline standards based on safety. • Recommendations from the FAA are implemented the world over. • It has responsibility for investigating US air crashes and is often called to help investigate overseas incidents, especially when US aircraft or airlines are involved. • Grants type certification to new aircraft based on rigorous testing.
International Air Transport Association (IATA)	Originally in 1919 but redrafted and received current name in 1945	Non Government Organisation (NGO) – Trade Body	• Representative group for international airline industry • Created standardisation through ticketing and three letter codes • Helps airlines become more profitable, safe and efficient. • Provides training and expertise in areas such as the environment
International Civil Aviation Organisation (ICAO)	1947	Inter Governmental Organisation (IGO) – Part of the United Nations	• Development of technical standards based on safety, security and environment. • Acts as a coordinator between IGO's and NGO's within Aviation • Creates international aviation legislation

Task 1

Look at the websites for the International Civil Aviation Organisation and the International Air Transport Association. From the information provided, how similar are the objectives of these two organisations and in what ways do you believe their agendas are dissimilar?

At a domestic level, airlines and airports are also subject to a number of regulatory and trade bodies. The main government department which has overall control for air transport is the Department for Transport (www.dft.gov.uk). It is this government department which is responsible for creating legislation and policy based on civil aviation. Planning applications are dealt with by this department taking into account environmental considerations. Part of the DFT's role is to investigate aircraft accidents in the UK or where a UK airliner is involved in an incident overseas – this work is undertaken by the Air Accident Investigation Branch (AAIB).Table 10.2 highlights the main organisations that have an influence of UK airline and airport operations.

Table 10.2 – UK Civil Aviation Organisations

Organisation	Date Established	Ownership	Role
Civil Aviation Authority (CAA)	1972	Public Corporation (QANGO) Revenue generated from services provided not by direct government funding	• Economic regulation of UK airports (BAA monopoly in particular) • Airspace policy formulation • Development and implementation of safety regulations • Protection of consumers through Air Travel Organiser's Licensing (ATOL) scheme • Represents passenger interests via the Air Transport Users' Council (AUC) • Maintains the UK aircraft register • Licences airports, aircraft and air crew • supervises medical regulations for air crew
National Air Traffic Service (NATS)	1962 founded as government department but was entrusted to a public/private partnership in 2003.	UK Government (49%), The Airline Group (42%), BAA (4%) and employees (5%)	• Provides airport ATC at 15 UK airports including LHR, LGW, STN, LTN, MAN, BHX, CWL, BRS and EDI • Provides ATC for all aircraft flying over UK airspace.

Conclusions

Although airlines are often free today to serve whichever city pairings they may choose, the commercial aviation industry still remains highly regulated in some respects due to the need to maintain high levels of safety and security. The role of public sector organisations has changed over the past three decades from being very hands on to one of monitoring and advising. This has allowed airlines and airports a certain amount of freedom to change the air product to best suit passenger needs.

References and Suggested Further Reading

Lawrence, H. (2004) Aviation and the Role of Government, Kendall / Hunt Publishing – (US Import)

Information regarding the role of the CAA and its CAP regulations can be found at www.caa.co.uk

Unit Eleven

Careers in Commercial Aviation

Unit Objectives:

On completing this unit, you should be able to:

- Comprehend the wide variety of jobs available within civil aviation
- Recognise the main sources of information and access to employment within commercial aviation
- Identify external factors which preclude employment opportunities within commercial aviation

Introduction

Commercial aviation offers a dynamic and intense employment opportunity with the ability in some cases to travel and, for most, to encounter cultures from across the globe on a daily basis. The number of people employed in commercial aviation in the UK totals over 700,000 (OEF, 2006) and within Europe the figure is an impressive 2.6 million (ATAG 2014) both directly and indirectly employed within the sector. The majority of people employed in commercial aviation will work for major airports or the larger airline operators. For example, British Airways employs 40,000 (BA 2015) staff in a variety of different roles from head office to cockpit and cabin crew. Some of the main reasons why people look to enter the industry are listed below:

- Dynamic environment to work in
- Ability to progress career quickly to management positions
- Seen as a glamorous industry to work in

The types of employment opportunity available within the sector vary with the type of organisation. Table 11.1 examines the different types of employment opportunities available within commercial aviation

Table 11.1 – Employment Opportunities Available within Commercial Aviation

Organisation	Employment Opportunities Available
Airline	Pilot
	Cabin Crew
	Dispatcher
	Station Manager
	Engineer
	Customer Service Agent
	Baggage Operatives
	Ramp Operatives
	Flight Operations
	Fleet Management
	Legal & Insurance Management
	Human Resource Management
	Reservation Agent
	Marketing
	Accounts and Finance
	Accounts Manager
	Air Cargo Agent
	Buyers
	IT Support and Systems
Airport	Airfield Operations
	Air Traffic Control
	Meteorologist
	Terminal Operations
	Passenger Information Assistant
	Duty Free Retail Assistant
	Check-in agent
	Security Agent
	Maintenance
	Legal & Insurance Management
	Human Resource Management
	Reservation Agent
	Marketing
	Buyers
	IT Support and Systems
	Planning and Policy
Public Sector	Air Traffic Control
	Meteorologist
	Customs and Immigration
	Police, Fire and Ambulance Service
	Pet Quarantine Inspector
	Passenger Survey Attendants (International Passenger Survey – UK)
Ground Handlers	Check-in
	Cleaning
	Catering
	Ramp Services
	Cargo Services
	Staff Transport

Source: Airline Websites, Aviation Job Search.com and FlightJobs.com

Task 1

Visit a website of an airline of your choice and look at their careers page. What are the main skills that are expected for a customer facing member of staff such as cabin crew or customer service agent?

Sources of Information for Commercial Aviation Employment

There are a number of information sources available to investigate employment opportunities within the commercial aviation sector. Probably, the best starting point, is to look at individual airline and airport websites. Here, for example, you will find a list of the latest vacancies that are available and the skills expected of you. Within the UK, companies such as British Airways, Virgin Atlantic and FlyBe all have current jobs advertised on their respective websites.

As with other areas of commercial aviation many airlines have outsourced their human resource requirements to specialist agencies. It is therefore useful to find out which agencies operate within your local airport as these may be a quicker and more positive way of getting onto the aviation employment ladder. At London Heathrow two of the biggest employment agencies are Face-to-Face Recruitment and HR in One.

There are also a number of websites which advertise current vacancies from airline and airport operators. The two main portals are www.aviationjobsearch.com and Flight Jobs (http://www.flightglobal.com/jobs/default.aspx). Both these sites offer the opportunity to upload your CV for respective employers to read.

The International Air Transport Association also offers a number of training courses and advice on its website as to how to enter the world of commercial aviation. As you are probably studying for a HND or Degree in Airline and Airport Management, the course information is not relevant but information on their intern programme may be of use.

Task 2

Visit www.aviationjobsearch.com. Make a list of the job categories available and then ask yourself which positions you think you will be able to apply for after you finish your higher education.

The Influence of External Factors on Employment Opportunities

The commercial aviation industry is currently recovering from a period of great uncertainty. At the time of writing (May 2015), airlines from Qantas to Ryanair have revised routes and in some cases reduced staff as a way of dealing with uncertain oil prices and the fall in consumer confidence due to a number of economic circumstances including the Eurozone crisis. Over the years, commercial aviation has been exposed to a number of external factors which have impacted on recruitment and employment levels. These past factors have included:-

- Oil crisis – The current level of oil has led to airlines introducing surcharges, grounding aircraft, cutting routes and lowering staffing levels as a way of reducing costs. A similar situation in the early 1970's left many airlines bankrupt, with the knock on effect of high levels of unemployment within the skilled commercial aviation workforce.

- Economic slowdowns – When the global economy or regional economies have entered recession, consumers tend to reduce their travelling habits. This in turn impacts on employment levels within the airlines that have to lay off staff to cope with reduced demand.

- Security fears – After the 9/11 attacks on New York, the commercial aviation industry was left reeling as bookings dried up as passengers feared to travel. This did cause over two years of stagnant bookings but has since recovered. The threat of terrorism is however, still with us and employment levels are dependant on what happens next.

- The SARS pandemic – The global nature of our community has also brought the risk of viruses travelling across the globe within hours and without detection until it is too late. Employment levels are again vulnerable based on future pandemic outbreaks.

- Environmental considerations – Perhaps more of a futuristic threat but a real one. Passengers are becoming more aware of the issues surrounding 'global warming' and the impact that aviation has on this. Passengers are therefore considering if flying is their best option. Whilst the future impact of these decisions has yet to be felt, it could potentially have implications for employment opportunities within commercial aviation.

Task 3

Investigate the ways in which Ryanair has looked to reduce the impact of oil price rises and the credit crunch on its operations.

Conclusions

The commercial aviation industry offers some excellent opportunities within a highly dynamic working environment. The skills required of any individual entering the market must include the ability to be flexible and to be able to work closely with customers to the point of being able to enhance any expectation they may have. The current economic climate may not be that bright, but most indicators point to the continued expansion of commercial aviation and therefore the employment opportunities within.

References and Suggested Further Reading

Air Transport Action Group – ATAG (2014) Aviation Benefits Beyond Borders Report - http://aviationbenefits.org/media/26786/ATAG__AviationBenefits2014_FULL_LowRes.pdf

Collins, V.R. (2002) Careers in Airlines and Airports, Kogan Page LTD.

Collins, V.R. (2004) Working in Aviation, Vacation Work Ltd.

Davis, S. (2005) Yes, You Can Be Cabin Crew! The Perfect Springboard to a new career as a cabin crew member: All the Inside Info You Need to Secure the Job of Your Dreams, Ready to Fly Publications.

Information on the IATA internship programme: http://www.iata.org/hc/iip.htm

Porter, A. (2004) So You Want to Be Air Cabin Crew? The In-depth Guide on How to Become a Cabin Crew Member, Travelvocation Books.

Rogers, C. (2008) How to Become Cabin Crew: An Aspiring Flight Attendant's Must Have Guide, CE Publishing.

Unit Twelve

The Future of Commercial Aviation

Unit Objectives:
On completing this unit, you should be able to:

- Explain the general trends that are occurring within commercial aviation
- Highlight the trends most likely to affect airline operations
- Discuss future commercial aircraft developments
- Highlight the key issues affecting airport operations

Introduction

Whilst it is impossible to predict future events or technology for that matter, it is necessary for commercial aviation strategist and planners to think what the future may hold. Aircraft technology is constantly progressing as are the airline products offered to passengers (as highlighted in unit six). With these factors in mind, the aim of this unit is to look into the near term and identify what trends may occur within the commercial aviation sector. To do this, the unit has been broken down into the three constituent parts of the industry, namely, Airlines, Airports and Commercial Aviation Manufacturers. The unit will first, however, explore the generic future trends that will impact on the commercial aviation industry.

Generic Future Trends

The main areas that are expected to affect the commercial aviation sector over the foreseeable future are as follows:-

- Environmental priorities will be pushed further up the agenda by environmentalists, governments and customers. The industry needs to be able to address these areas with a clear vision of how it will tackle engine emissions and aircraft noise. The creation of CleanSky and Enviro.aero has helped address some of these issues. The use of carbon offsetting programmes by airlines has also had a positive impact on customers.
- The global economic downturn has already started to impact on the industry and has seen the first casualties. These have mainly been niche players who have not been able to fall back on other routes or products to help offset market weaknesses. Silverjet, Maxjet and EOS are all carriers who tried to compete with the main scheduled airlines either based on price or product innovation. They were, however, unable to sustain the costs associated with higher fuel prices based on their average load factors.
- The downturn has created the first wave of consolidation within the industry. The highly publicised merger of Delta and Northwest Airlines / Continental and United will have a massive impact on both domestic and intercontinental flights to the US. This merger has forced the hand of American Airlines that filed for Anti-Trust Immunity resulting in its merger with US Airways.

- Price will be another key factor within the sector. Low Cost airlines will continue to battle for customers on the short haul routes which will create further consolidation. Airports that have relied on the low cost product will have to respond to these price challenges to make sure that they keep their route network. Ryanair, for example, has a history of pulling out of airports where the economics were seen as being unfavourable. This, in turn, will have a knock on impact for aircraft manufacturers. Currently, their order books are full but as has been proven in past downturns these can suddenly dry up as orders are cancelled or deferred. This will require aircraft manufacturers to look closely at their order books as to which airlines are likely to see through their commitments and those that are likely to cancel. The price of aircraft will thus be affected by any major downturn or will it? Many believe that the need for more environmentally favourable aircraft will only help manufacturers during the downturn based on the economic efficiencies such equipment will bring.
- The continued trend towards online booking and e-Ticketing will have further negative consequences for retail travel agents. Disintermediation will continue as airlines have cut commission rates to zero in an attempt to attract more customers to their own websites for booking flights and other ancillary products.

Airline Future Trends

The airline product is becoming far more high tech and it is this trend which will continue into the near future. Airlines have already had notable success in converting customers from booking at travel agents to direct online booking. Furthermore, airlines have been able to develop databases of passenger preferences and their travelling habits, such as their favourite seat and time of flight through frequent flyer schemes and through customer online check-in systems. The technology that powers these systems is allowing airlines to develop mobile phone/PDA check-in facilities as well as issuing e-tickets to these mobile devices.

Technology is also at the core of the in-flight product with development of sophisticated entertainment systems. A number of airlines have introduced live TV while others have introduced internet access via satellite technology. These developments are set to continue as passengers are offered even greater technology access at seat, from editing their holiday videos from their personal media console to ordering drinks and food whilst messaging their friend to update them of arrival time.

Airport Future Trends

The constraints of airports are becoming all too apparent within the UK and other destinations. London Heathrow is full and is looking to build a new runway to help ease congestion. London Stansted has also submitted planning applications for a new terminal and runway. For airports, the future is not just about expanding to keep pace with growth but the renewal of existing facilities to bring them into line with customer expectations. Here, the regeneration of London Heathrow is a classic example of how, with the aid of new facilities, an airport has been able to look at its provision and regenerate, as airlines have been moved from one terminal to another. Failure to do this will see even more passengers bypassing Heathrow and instead flying to Amsterdam (AMS) or Paris (CDG) or Frankfurt (FRA) to connect with their onward destinations.

For the world's most popular airports, the lack of landing and takeoff places (slots) will have further consequences. For airlines to sustain services into such airports, the routes will need to have a high profit profile which can only be achieved mostly via long haul operations. Therefore, concern has been raised by commentators including Bob Ayling (ex CEO of British Airways) that such airports may not contribute greatly to the local and national economies as they will rely heavily on transit passengers who contribute little directly to the hub airports national economy. This argument is, however, countered by the airports, including BAA, who state that without transit passengers the airports route structure would not be as diverse or sustainable.

Technological developments will also have an impact on airports. The development of RFID and Bluetooth facilities will allow airports to track and deliver an even higher level of baggage on-time. The trend to give passengers even greater information on their flight, such as gate updates and final boarding times, through their mobile devices, will be expected by airlines. These developments will also allow them with the aid of CCTV to track passengers and profile them with greater accuracy as they move through the system.

Airports also need to think about information provision as more and more passengers have access to laptop computers and PDA's. Here, the use of free or credit based Wi-Fi and even further into the future WiMax facilities, are essential.

Commercial Aviation Manufacturers Future Trends

Aircraft manufacturers such as Boeing have, over the past decade, turned their attention away from designing high speed craft such as the Sonic Cruiser, to concentrate instead on developing high tech derivatives of current jet designs. The Boeing 787 is a good example of an aircraft which through the use of composite materials, computer aided design and great performance improvements from power plants has helped transform its environmental and economic ratings.

Task

Based on these future trends which sector of commercial aviation faces the biggest challenges and why?

Conclusions

The future trends for the commercial aviation industry offer both challenges and opportunities. One thing is for certain it is one of the most exciting and entertaining sector to be employed in for the foreseeable future. Aircraft technology has pushed the boundaries of development, but continues to strive for quiet and efficient aircraft to meet the challenges of today and tomorrow. Airlines are constantly looking to improve their product so as to attract, as well as maintain customers, which leads to its own challenges. Airports face similar competitive confrontations as the new generation of airlines tends to be more mobile than their predecessors.

References and Suggested Further Reading

Bob Ayling 3rd Heathrow runway comments from Sunday Times 4th May 2008: http://www.timesonline.co.uk/tol/comment/columnists/guest_contributors/article3867768.ece

For information on what IATA as a trade body are undertaking with regards to environmental issues log onto: http://www.enviro.aero